TRANSITION

One Kid's Bank Shot to the NFL

This book is a memoir, chronicled and written prior to 2014 as a collection of the author's thoughts and experiences. It depicts details and events as the author remembers them and may be remembered differently by others.

bright sky press
HOUSTON, TEXAS

2365 Rice Blvd., Suite 202
Houston, Texas 77005

ISBN: 978-1-942945-51-2

10 9 8 7 6 5 4 3 2 1

Library of Congress Cataloging-in-Publication Data on file with the publisher.

Editorial Director: Lauren Gow
Editor: Lucy Herring Chambers
Designer: Marla Y. Garcia

Printed in Canada through Friesens

TRANSITION

One Kid's Bank Shot to the NFL

FENDI ONOBUN

 **bright sky press**

HOUSTON, TEXAS

To James Onobun

Thank you Dad! Love you.

TABLE OF
CONTENTS

Prologue **6**

CHAPTER 1: 20/20 .... **13**

CHAPTER 2: Bigger Than Me **19**

CHAPTER 3: Football? **29**

CHAPTER 4: How Sweet It Is **43**

CHAPTER 5: A New Road **51**

CHAPTER 6: Tryna' Go Pro **55**

CHAPTER 7: Dream Deferred **63**

CHAPTER 8: Crossroads **71**

CHAPTER 9: Decisions... Decisions **79**

CHAPTER 10: Clarity **87**

CHAPTER 11: For Love or Money **93**

CHAPTER 12: H-Town Bound **111**

CHAPTER 13: Two-A-Days **129**

CHAPTER 14: Growing Pains **143**

CHAPTER 15: The Season **151**

CHAPTER 16: Practicing Patience **159**

CHAPTER 17: Settling In **165**

CHAPTER 18: Tryna' Go Pro—Again **189**

CHAPTER 19: Pro Day 2.0 .... **207**

CHAPTER 20: Closer To My Dream **217**

CHAPTER 21: My Moment **233**

Epilogue **243**

Acknowledgements **246**

PROLOGUE

I had done it what seemed like a million times before. But, for some reason, tonight felt different.

Walking down the corridor underneath Houston's Toyota Center, I felt the buzz building, although doors wouldn't open for another three hours. Headphones and shades made me look calm and collected, but my heart was about to pop right out of my suit.

The moment I had waited for throughout the off-season had just gotten a little bit closer.

As the staff members opened the double doors, I said my hellos. Over the music blaring through my headphones, I heard the familiar metal-on-metal clang, the inconspicuous entrance into a whole different world, the NBA locker room.

I walked over to my locker, fourth slot on the left, and sat down in my chair. A variety of pre-game routines surrounded me. Some players listened to music, some went to the training room for heat or tape, and others watched ESPN or game film on their iPads. Everyone had his own way of preparing for competition.

I was no different. I turned my chair around and stared at the contents of my locker for a moment. In perfect condition, my number 21 uniform hung on the right side, placed with precision. Opposite my jersey, in the lower left corner, my Nikes™ sat together with military exactitude, my NBA socks neatly tucked inside. My red arm sleeve dangled above them on a hook. Everything I needed was perfectly arranged down to my pack of Stride gum sitting in the upper-right-hand corner next to my orange Gatorade™.

That spot, fourth slot on the left from the double-door entrance, was my safe haven.

In the midst of everything else going on in my life, I could get in my zone there. No matter what was happening around me, it was the space for my mental rehearsal, the place where I envisioned what I was going to do in the game.

In that space, every shot I took went in, and every rebound was mine. There wasn't a miss in my world. I didn't envision anyone stopping me but myself.

Everything was ready to go. It was time.

Coach stressed to us in the locker room that our opponents were coming off a good year. Our advantage over this team was speed. As he talked and the tip-off clock wound down, I was putting on my pre-game shorts, well into my routine.

"Fifty minutes before tip off!"

That was my cue. I headed to the court to get a few shots up alone before the game. Headphones on, still in my zone, I walked out of the tunnel.

The buttery sweet aroma of carnival snacks instantly hit my nose. The concession stands had just started preparing food for the crowd, and the rich smells covered the court.

Fans trickled down the aisles, and the stadium was filling up quickly. I went through my pre-game warm-up: stretch, a light jog to get my blood flowing, and a quick game of around the world with one of the ball boys as my rebounder. I put up about 125 shots and worked on a few of my moves before jogging back into the locker room to dress for the game.

Walking into the locker room, right on schedule I heard, "Twenty-five minutes before tip off!"

Back in my safe haven, I anticipated what was to come, now only minutes away. I pulled my uniform over my head, fixed my arm sleeve, adjusted my socks and laced my Nikes™ a tad tighter.

The team gathered one last time before taking the floor.

With each step I took towards that tunnel, electric excitement flowed through my body. My ears boomed with the screams of twenty thousand fans, cheering at the top their lungs for us.

I was surprised to realize I wasn't nervous. All I felt was an adrenaline rush.

I could tell by how high I was jumping every time I went up for a dunk; every shot I put up went in: it was going to be a good night.

The horn buzzed.

The lights cut out.

As fireworks exploded above the basket, I felt like I was at a concert. I could feel the heat from the torch as it threw blueish-orange flames from the court. I ripped off my warm-ups and took a seat at our bench while the pre-game video and player introductions were being done. Nerves tried to crawl into me, but I remained stoic, focused.

The moment had arrived.

"At small forward, from the University of Arizona, *num*-ber *twen*-ty-*one*! *Fen*-di-i-i *O-no*-bun!"

The crowd erupted! I jumped out of my seat and, with a slow creep of low-fives, headed down the lane to give my teammate at the end an elevated chest bump. I was so prepared for this moment. As I slammed against him, I felt like I hung in the air forever.

We huddled up at center court. "Alright, fellas, let's go out here and do what we *do*! It's *our* time! Let's show the city what we got this year! *Win three*! One, two, three: *Win*!"

The lights cut back on. Smoke from the fireworks drifted above us. Anticipation from the fans surrounded the court, pulsing as the referee walked towards center court for the opening tip off.

The ref tossed the jump ball.

The ball was tapped towards me. Before the defender could get his hands on it, I grabbed it, and gave it to our point guard. He signaled the play, and I ran down the right side of the baseline to get into my spot.

Our center and power forward moved towards me. They set double picks for me on the baseline to trap my defender. I came off the screen and curled around it towards the basket.

As I was coming off the screen, the point guard passed me the ball. I had both defenders follow me, which left the center open. When he became free, he went towards the basket as the open man.

I lobbed the ball up by the rim for an easy dunk. He caught it about a foot and a half above the rim and slammed it home.

The crowd went wild! The play couldn't have been executed any better.

On defense, we rebounded off their miss, and our guard hit me with a pass on the right wing in transition for an open three.

Swish! Nothing but net!

We were on a roll, and the fans were going crazy! I was all smiles, running back down the court holstering my hands with the three-ball sign. With our speed, their mistakes were killing them, and we got out to a quick 9-0 run.

We turned up our defense and got a steal. I took off running down the left wing and was able to catch the outlet pass a few feet behind the three-point line. I took two dribbles on the move and jumped from the middle of the lane—a Lebron-esque tomahawk slam!

I posed in the air for all the cameramen on the floor. *Boom!*

"*Ah-h-h-h-h-h-h-h-h!*" I screamed in excitement.

We were on an 11-0 run, and the other team called time out. I had five of the last eleven points with an assist. The crowd chanted, "FEN-DI! FEN-DI! FEN-DI!"

FEN-DI! FEN-DI! FEN-DI!

"Fen-di, Fendi! Wake up!" I felt a nudge on my shoulder. "Hey, buddy, your surgery went great. We were able to salvage and repair your tendon fully. You're on your way to recovery."

What?

Wait... had I been dreaming? The game had felt so real.

"What's wrong? You sound confused." I opened my eyes and recognized Doctor Kaplan, the team's orthopaedist I had seen just before I went under the anesthesia.

"Oh, nothing. Nothing's wrong," I told him. "I was dreaming, I guess. Dang, it felt so real. Doc, I was hooping, like playing basketball! I was in a game and we were on an 11-0 run; it was the season opener! I could have sworn I was actually playing the way that dream felt."

Doc chuckled. "The anesthesia got to ya a little bit, huh? Well your knee is on its way to recovery. The tough part is done. Everything went smoothly during the surgery. Rehab starts next week."

I lay on a hospital bed in the recovery room staring at the fluorescent ceiling light. I had IV tubes connected to me, and all I heard was the obnoxious beep of the monitor that tracked my blood pressure.

Reality sunk in.

I could see the bulge of my bandaged leg through the thin hospital covers. My leg felt like it was in a cast, but I knew it was just thoroughly wrapped. I couldn't move it, let alone feel it. But I knew once the medication wore off I was going to be in pain.

I looked around the room and sighed. A worn phrase came into my head: "the life of an athlete."

Before the surgery, my wife, Stephanie, had said, "It'll be okay. You'll get through this, just like all the other obstacles you've endured in your life. You'll make it through this one, too!"

This was my third knee surgery in my five-year career and probably the toughest injury to date. Thinking about the repaired rupture in my knee, I laid my head back on the pillow and closed my eyes. I drifted back into that awesome dream that Doc had interrupted.

It felt so real.

It was my childhood dream come true.

All I ever wanted to do was play in the NBA.

CHAPTER 1

2O/2O

THE CLOCK'S WINDING DOWN, *and the game is on the line. Onobun has the ball. He drives to the hoop… 3… 2… he pulls up for the shot—*
"Fendi!"
Clank!

My dad stuck his head out the door and asked, "Don't you have to get ready for school? Is all your homework finished?"

The basketball bounced off the back of the rim and rolled down the driveway. I couldn't even get my game-winning shot off without his interruption.

"Yes it is, Dad," I said, trotting inside the house to get ready for school.

Basketball was my first love. I first picked up a ball when I was three years old. By age six, my eyes were

Showing off my first basketball trophy, winter 1995.

glued to the TV, soaking up my favorite Chicago Bulls player, Michael Jordan.

What kid with hoop dreams didn't do that?

I didn't start playing competitively until I was seven. Basketball was an escape for me. I thought about it and dreamed about it constantly, because it provided me a place to get away.

My childhood had been complicated and basketball kept me stable.

"Poops?" my mother called as she opened the door to my room. She always called me "Poopsie," which she shortened to "Poops," and I couldn't stand it.

My eyes barely open. She called out again, "Wake up, Poops, we're going to the beach!"

"Beach?" I asked in excitement. "Really?!" This was my wish come true! I screamed and jumped out of my bed to get ready for the beach. I was so happy!

My mother, who preferred to be called "Dee," always told me that we'd go to the beach one day. I had never been before, but I had always wondered what it would be like. Finally, three days after my seventh birthday, the day had come.

I didn't know what to expect. Whenever I saw the beach on TV it looked like so much fun. All I could think about was how big my sand castle would be and what it would feel like swimming in the waves.

I couldn't wait!

"Dee, do they have a basketball court there?" I asked as I scrambled to get ready.

"Yes! They sure do. Bring your ball, and pack up your things," she said. "We're going to Galveston to celebrate your birthday!" I quickly grabbed my flip-flops, swimming trunks, my basketball, and a beach towel and then scrambled around my room to look for my shades. My mind was going crazy. I wanted to teleport to the sand that instant.

"Here, pack your things in this, Poops." Dee said. "And bring your Nintendo." She left an empty comforter bag in my room.

I looked at it, confused. *Why do I need this big ole bag to pack for the beach?* I thought to myself. *And why do I need my game at the beach?*

It was weird, but she was my mom. I did what she said. I dropped my towel, flip-flops, my video game and a few toys I could play with into the bag.

I sat on the bed next to my basketball, ready for the beach.

"Fendi, you're going to be late for school! Get off the bed, we have to go!" my dad said.

By the age of twelve, I was waking up early every morning, shooting hoops before school. Every morning ended the same: Dad calling me in to get ready for school.

My father, James Onobun, was a strict disciplinarian. He valued education and hard work.

"Fendi, read your books! And study hard!" he always said to me.

He was born and raised in Nigeria and had been brought up very differently from the "American way," as he always told me. He came to the United States on a soccer scholarship with nothing but a few dollars in his pocket. He made the most of what he had, and he created a life for himself.

He taught me the importance of diligence, education, perseverance, and respect. That was his doctrine, the words he would have written on a family crest if he had one. He made sure to instill the same values in me.

My Dad (Left) James Eromosele Onobun

His main concern for me was never athletics, or my dream of going to the NBA.

My father cared about my schoolwork, my character, and a secure future based on the foundation of education; anything else was secondary. School was first, always.

Although he had gotten me involved in competitive basketball, if my grades weren't good, he'd pull me out of hoops.

As a kid, making it to the NBA and playing for the Houston Rockets was my biggest goal in life. But I knew if my grades weren't right, Dad wouldn't let me play. There was nothing else I wanted more, so I made sure I took care of business in school.

In the summer after sixth grade, I hit a growth spurt. At thirteen, by the time seventh grade started, I was six-foot-three. Seventh grade was the first year students in Texas could compete competitively in school sports. Out of pure excitement I played three sports: football, basketball, and track.

7th grade basketball team photo. O'Donnell Middle School. Alief, Texas 1999.

I had never tried football or track before, but I was a decent athlete and I did pretty well. Basketball was my clear favorite.

By the time I was in eighth grade, I started playing AAU basketball. The rest was history. I focused on hoops because I was clear about my goal: I wanted to play in the NBA.

(First year playing football) 7th grade football photo. O'Donnell Middle School. Alief, Texas 1999.

As a high school standout basketball player, I played all over the country during the summer. The select traveling team, the Houston Hoops, provided me with the opportunity to play against some of the best basketball players in the nation.

When I reached this level, I knew I was on the path to reach my dreams, but I still had a long way to go. I had to make a lot of sacrifices, but nothing made me happier than playing the sport I loved.

AAU Team Houston Hoops. Top 5 10th grade team in the country. Summer 2002.

By the time I was a sophomore in high school, colleges from around the country were recruiting me. By 10th grade, several colleges had offered me a ticket to a free education.

It was crazy how fast it was all coming together. I had dedicated so much of my time to basketball since the day my dad first used it as a tool to keep me busy as a child. My love for the game and the time I had spent practicing was finally paying off in the direction I had imagined.

School Sports **magazine cover. Spring 2005, senior year.**

The spring of my junior year, I accepted a basketball scholarship to the University of Arizona. I wanted to make it to the NBA, and Arizona felt like the stepping-stone to get there. I knew it would be tough, but I had made it this far and had no plans of looking back.

I was going to do my thing in college, get a degree, then go pro.

There were only a few of us that made it out of Alief, TX. I wanted to be one of the ones who said "I made it."

CHAPTER 2

BIGGER THAN ME

As a kid, another thing I enjoyed was playing video games. But no matter the game, there was always a menu bar that read "Options."

At the time, I didn't know the exact definition of the word. What I *did* know was that the options tab gave me different ways to play the game the way *I* wanted to play it.

As a rising senior at the University of Arizona in the summer of 2009, I had a couple options available to me. It was time for me to make some major decisions about the future. As graduation approached, I asked myself almost daily, "What am I going to do with my life? Where am I going to go?"

I didn't know how anything was going to play out.

Looking back, I remember how wild it felt that I had even gotten to that point. My life seemed to change within the blink of an eye. One minute I was a kid scrolling through the options of a video game, and the next I had to make serious decisions about my life's future.

I was grateful enough to be in a position where I even had options, but as much as I wanted to make a good decision, I had no idea which option to choose.

My dad's two biggest messages to me were: *The decisions you make today, lead to the life you live* and *Fight the "good fight" and endure the race.* Now, at this crossroads in my life, I had fought and endured; and I knew that, whatever decision I made, I'd have to live with it and live in it.

I also knew God had a plan for me. But being in the unknown frightened me. Life's options aren't as easy as a video game, and there is no "restart" button; we live with the decisions we make.

My dad's favorite sayings had never felt so relevant. My time at the University of Arizona would be coming to an end in less than a year. I couldn't believe I was actually wrapping up my four years of basketball there, and I wasn't sure if my dream of going pro would actually become a reality.

Would I ever play basketball at a higher level?

Only time would tell.

Four years before this crossroads, I had been a five-star basketball recruit from Alief Taylor High School in Houston, Texas. I was a *good* player; but I knew choosing to go to Arizona would only make me *better.* I was going to be playing for a national powerhouse basketball program under Hall of Fame coach Lute Olson for the next four years.

What seventeen-year-old basketball junkie wouldn't want an opportunity like that? I was getting a free education while attending one of the finest collegiate basketball schools in the nation. I couldn't have felt any better. It had taken a lot of hard work and was extremely difficult, but I had made it to the highest level of collegiate hoops.

I had followed a dream and stayed the course.

When I got to Zona, the competition was everything I expected. Our practices were filled with future NBA players, future overseas pros, and highly talented hoopers. That was the environment; I was playing against the best, every single day.

Despite my natural talents, I wasn't able to sustain a consistent position in the rotation throughout my career. It just didn't happen. My freshman and junior years were probably my best. Sophomore year, I seriously considered transfer-

Freshman year at U of A. 2005-2006 season. *Photo courtesy of University of Arizona Athletics*

ring, and senior year was probably the most memorable, but I was ready for it to be over. Overall, it was a roller coaster: I went from sixth man, to the bench mob, to a few starts, to sometimes feeling like a walk-on. There were some highs, and a lot of lows, but it surely was not the way I had imagined my career would go.

Freshman year, the coaching staff decided to red-shirt me. I wasn't happy about it, but I understood. Partly, it made me feel like I wasn't good enough to play, although logically I knew I was.

Despite being put on the shelf that year, I was still part of the team. I just didn't compete in games—our practices were my games. It made me sick not playing, but it was a time for me to get better.

The decision motivated me. It motivated me to improve: I had never worked as hard as I did my freshman year. It was a level beyond high school. That year I improved so much the coaching staff decided to pull my redshirt halfway through the season, and I played for the remainder of the year.

For a lot of reasons, the jury was still out on the move, but I wanted to play. I wanted to do what I went there for: hoop and to give myself a chance to go to the league.

As focused as I was on becoming a better ball player at Arizona, little did I know the pulled redshirt would forever change the trajectory of my athletic career.

Coming off my freshman year as the sixth man, I thought I was in a good place to build on what I had started. We had such a good team—we finished the year with twenty wins and made it to the second round of the NCAA Tournament.

It was a great year for me, going from redshirt freshman to the team's most improved player. My future looked bright, and I only saw myself getting better year after year.

During the remaining three years, I experienced three coaching changes, new systems, and injuries that kept me sidelined or out of the rotation. We also reloaded with fresh talent every year.

Sophomore year at U of A. 2006-2007 season. *Photo courtesy of University of Arizona Athletics*

Yes, I was playing for a top-tier basketball program, but 2006 to 2009 were the most tumultuous years the UA program had ever suffered since before the Olson era began. After my sophomore season, I was basically one foot out the door.

But my father encouraged me to stay: to hold on to the commitment I made, to keep fighting, to keep working, and to endure the race. As much as I personally didn't want to hear that, my faith kept me there.

I believed God wanted me to stay put at Arizona. I didn't understand it, and I wanted to leave, but something in my spirit told me there was something greater to be gained from staying. I finished out my remaining two years at Arizona.

By the time I was a senior, a lot had changed. Coach Olson had retired after twenty-five years with the program. We had an interim coach for the second season in a row, and things were just different.

This was my last go-round. I was hopeful for a solid senior season. I had been there as long as anyone on the team. I was a leader, and we were young.

We probably had two NBA-ready players on our roster that year, and I wasn't one of them. Did I lose hope in my dream that year? Not necessarily, but I just didn't see the opportunity I had when I had come in as a freshman.

Senior year at U of A. Winter 2008. *Photo Courtesy of University of Arizona Athletics.*

I had ability, and I knew I could play; but at this point of my life, I wanted to take the season one day at a time and enjoy each moment, because I knew the end was near. I told myself I'd worry about my next move once the season was over.

Nonetheless, it was hard to not feel the pressure of what my future held—the approaching moment was inevitable. That year on the floor I was our "energy guy," a spark off the bench. I'd come into the game, grab a few rebounds, play tough defense, set screens—I was that guy. I was "blue collar." I weighed around 245 lbs. that year, the heaviest I had ever played, but I knew it was a role that needed to be filled.

It was upsetting that my career had been so different than my initial vision for it. Although I had recommitted myself mentally before my junior season, there were still times when I did not want to be at Arizona. It felt like I had made a mistake.

I was often told that God had a plan. In the midst of all the change and uncertainty, it was hard for me to see. But whenever I took my own feelings out of the equation and just thought about the situation, I realized how God had used me that year.

One thing that I truly needed to understand, that I didn't always grasp at the time, was that the situation was bigger than me.

Every game I led our team in our pre-game prayer. Once a week I held Bible study at my apartment. Often teammates came to me for advice on how to balance school and basketball. In games I would see things other players didn't and would help them understand certain aspects of the collegiate game.

It was bigger than me; I had to understand that and make that sacrifice. In my locker that year I had a scripture written on paper: *He must increase, but I must decrease. John 3:30.* It was a constant reminder to me. Whatever role I filled my senior year, I knew that I was an example.

I had to help my team any way I could, because it wasn't about me.

In sports, it's hard not to characterize leadership through numbers and statistics, but I knew it was my intellect and experience that would help the team the most. I knew what to expect. I had learned how to sacrifice for the betterment of the team, and the more faith I put in Him, the less I'd worry about me. I understood the highs and lows of a collegiate season—it was my fourth rodeo in Tucson.

What I didn't know was whether or not I'd be fulfilling my childhood dream the following year. Matter of fact, that dream had never felt so far away as it did at that moment. It felt like such a long shot.

After a particularly hard practice my senior year, all the other players had cleared out of the locker room. I sat in my locker, deflated, staring ahead.

What could possibly be next for me?

"Poops, let's go!" Dee called. "Are all your things packed? The taxi's outside waiting for us!"

"BEACH TIME!" I screamed, dragging my heavy bag to the door. "How long does it take to get to Galveston, Dee?"

"We'll be there soon. Grab your things," she said.

We walked down the stairs from our apartment, put our bags in the trunk of the taxi, and zoomed away from the building. I waved at the security guard as the taxi driver checked us out of the complex. We were one step closer to the beach!

Dee wasn't talking, so I had plenty of time to think on the ride. *Why are we taking so much stuff?* I wondered again. But I figured we were staying for the whole weekend, so I put that thought out of my head. I was just excited to finally be going to the beach.

"How long are we staying there?" I asked, wanting to talk about this wonderful journey.

My mother didn't respond.

Maybe we can stay a week! I thought to myself. I didn't know. But under my enthusiasm, other feelings were rising. Yes, this was fun, but it was fishy at the same time. I had wanted to go to the beach for so long, and we had never gone. *Why now? Why all this stuff?*

When I had packed up the big bag, I wrote a note. It simply said, "Dad, we are going to the beach –Fendi."

I hid it under the kitchen sink. Something just didn't seem right, even from the beginning.

The taxi ride was a long one, and I dozed off. I woke to the driver's voice. "Alright ma'am. Here we are."

I woke up and looked out the window. We were at a station. "Why are we here? Is this how we get to the beach?" I asked.

"Let's go!" Dee said, pulling me out of the taxi. There were huge white buses with blue dogs painted on the side of them and GREYHOUND written in big letters. People were everywhere, going in and out of doors at the station with bags of all sorts.

I stood by the curb, looking around in confusion.

"Poops, let's *go!*" She put my bag into my hands and pulled me along by my sleeve.

"Where's the beach?" I kept asking, but I was not getting any answers. *Maybe this is how we get there,* I told myself, though no one in the big station looked like they were headed on vacation.

Dee led me to a counter where they gave her some tickets. Then we walked over to one of the big buses and dropped our bags with a guy standing by the bus doors. We went onto the bus and found two seats on the right-hand side towards the middle.

I looked at Dee, and she just stared straight ahead, not answering my questions. All I wanted to do was go to the beach. I didn't know which beach we were going to or when I'd get there. So many things seemed weird.

I started to wonder if we were even going to a beach at all.

In spite of my overall unhappiness and the challenge of trying to not worry about what the future held, being strong in my faith carried me through my final year at Arizona.

I thanked God daily for guiding me through my confusion. It was tough to feel so high at one point and then so low at another, to recommit myself and have my expectations not met. But I kept praying and thinking of my dad's wisdom: *That's life, full of highs and lows. It's what you do with those highs and lows that make you who you are.*

I was fortunate enough to have people in my circle who kept me encouraged when things got difficult. I was going to receive my bachelor's degree in May, and, realistically, I knew the NBA was a long shot. But I still felt like I was stripped of my first love. I had to constantly remind myself that God had a plan, no matter how much or how little I played in games. He was ordering my steps.

One of the people who always tried to keep my spirits up was my friend Keith Rosenblatt. During my freshman year I had met Keith, his wife Suzette, and their two little boys, Luc and Bret. Before the games, Luc and Bret would wait by our tunnel to give me a high five before going to their seats. I was their favorite player on the team.

It was a good feeling to know a couple of young kids in Tucson looked up to me. Keith told me, "If my kids like ya, I like ya."

That was the start of a friendship that would play a big part in my life.

CHAPTER 3

FOOTBALL?

At Arizona it almost seemed like the norm for guys to head to the NBA. Their NCAA careers would come to an end, then in June they would get drafted. That's how good of a basketball program it was.

In my tenure, I saw seven of my Wildcat teammates get drafted—which was a lot for one program in just four years. The ones who didn't go to the NBA had an opportunity to play professionally overseas.

I hadn't heard from an agent all year; NBA scouts weren't looking at me, or asking about me. I prayed so much. I kept getting the message that everything was going to be OK, but it was very hard to hold still.

Keith had a good friend, Billy Seymour, who I met at the end of my junior year. Billy was about 6'3", 225 lbs. He had played tight end at the University of Michigan from 1997–2001 and had a short stint with the Green Bay Packers.

When I met Billy, he was long removed from his NFL days. He worked as a pharmaceutical sales rep for Striker full-time, but he still volunteered as a coach at a high school in Tucson. The first time Billy saw me his eyes lit up, and he said, "Jeez, kid, you look like a football player! You ever thought of playing football?"

I laughed. I figured he would say that, considering he was a football coach.

At the time, I was still recovering from a stress fracture surgery in my left leg, so all my workouts were upper-body lifts. I was a little bigger than my playing size, but I definitely didn't take him seriously.

As time passed, I developed a pretty good relationship with Billy through Keith. They were always in my ear about football—not forcefully, but it was a topic they never shied away from.

I didn't even *like* football. I didn't watch it, nor did I understand it. I hadn't played it since seventh grade! All I had wanted to do since I was twelve was play basketball. It baffled me how much these two guys tried to convince me to play a sport I didn't even know.

I never entertained their football shenanigans, but from time to time I would joke around with them about it. But really… football? They had to know I wasn't actually serious.

The whole summer it seemed like they were on a tag-team chase to get me thinking about football. So much so that by my senior year it didn't sound like a bad alternative. From all the upper body lifting I had done over the summer, I was a solid 245 lbs., which helped them convince me to give it a shot.

"Fendi you're 6'6", 245 lbs., and you make all your teammates look like string beans! You are the perfect size for an end!" Billy would tell me. And people on the court had said to me that I looked like a football player. But it was crazy to me.

Basketball was my game. I hadn't lost my love for it, but I was really starting to wonder if it loved me back.

With only seven or eight games left in my senior season, the end was near, very

Senior year at U of A. 2008-2009 season. *Photo courtesy of University of Arizona Athletics*

near. As a last-chance effort to get better and relieve some stress, I would shoot in the practice gym late at night. It was therapeutic for me. I knew if I got up shots, my shooting would improve, and so would my confidence, and my game. But I still wasn't playing much, and I hated it.

Keith more than anyone understood my frustrations. As the season dwindled, he was the one who kept my spirits up.

One day after a light conference-game practice, I called him. I needed a change, something different. "Hey! What are you doing now? I asked. I didn't even give him time to respond. "How about you, Billy, and I go play catch somewhere?"

"Really?" he said, in complete shock.

"Yeah, why not? I need another stress reliever. You know, just get away and try something new. Why not football?"

I met Keith and Billy that afternoon at Catalina Foothills High School to shoot the breeze and play catch. It wasn't much more than that. I was just having fun, like a kid throwing the ball with his dad.

"Well, he can catch!" Billy said to Keith after we had thrown around for a while.

"That's a good thing," Keith answered.

I kept working hard at practice but things didn't change as far as playing time. Although I had come to accept that I wouldn't be in the NBA, I believed I'd be playing professionally overseas. I just needed to get through this last little bit of the year. I kept my faith, worked hard, and rode the season out as best I could.

I was now playing catch with Billy and Keith almost three times a week after practice. It helped me get my mind off of my frustrations about basketball. It provided a getaway, a change-up—and it was kind of fun.

I knew football was something I didn't want to pursue; however, the change of scenery felt good. A lot of other people were in my ear telling me I should play football, too. But I didn't understand all the fuss. I kept moving towards whatever part of my basketball dreams I could salvage.

Toward the final stretch of conference play, our team hit a really bad losing streak. After winning seven games in a row, we lost four straight. Our chance to make it into the NCAA Tournament was in jeopardy.

Arizona had been to the Big Dance for twenty-four consecutive years, and the program was on the brink of breaking the longest NCAA Tourney appearance streak in the country. That was a big deal. We didn't want to be known as the team that broke the streak. We had to focus on winning our last regular-season game to even give ourselves a chance.

After going out a few more times with Keith and Billy, I was beginning to look forward to playing catch with them. I became more familiar with the football. I looked at our outings as a great way to take me away from the sour feelings I was having on the hardwood.

After just a few meetings at the park, Billy had already analyzed me.

"Fendi, you're a natural athlete with a lot of raw talent and good hands. I'm telling ya, kid, this could be somethin'."

He and Keith started really trying to convince me to give football a shot. It had been just about three weeks now that I had been playing catch with them. They kept stressing that I should at least "try it out."

I was still thinking these guys were crazy, but the idea was becoming more enticing.

One afternoon, instead of ignoring their talk, I asked, "Y'all think I could do this for real, man?"

"Uh, *yes!*" they both responded.

Later that same week, the craziest thing happened. Completely out of this world. Coach Ed, the head strength and conditioning coach for our football team, told me that an NFL scout had inquired about me. He said the scout had seen me lifting in the weight room and wondered if I could play football.

I was shocked when Coach told me that. *Me?* I thought. *I'm not a football player. Do I seriously look like one?* Division I football players train most of their lives to get to where they are—just like I had with basketball.

Then Coach Ed recommended that I participate in the football team's annual pro day. This was where the Wildcats' pro prospects and graduating seniors perform a series of drills in front of NFL scouts to determine if they have what it takes to play in the league.

"Are you serious?" I asked Coach.

"Yes, I'm dead serious," he said. "Just come out."

We had four games left in a span of three weeks. I wasn't sure if I could do it, because the date of the pro day was the same date as our Pac-10 Tournament in Los Angeles.

Coach Ed told me that I could work out for the scouts at a later date in April with another guy who was coming off of an injury.

The later April date would give me the extra time to prepare. I *wasn't* sure if I wanted to play football; I *was* sure it wouldn't hurt to try.

When I shared this news with Keith, Billy, my dad, and a few close friends, they all said, "Do it!"

After all the frustrations of hoops, the weeks of playing catch, and this lingering idea of trying football, this scout who inquired about me put the icing on the cake.

Why not?

Despite all the football talk, these last four regular season games were critical for us if the streak was going to continue. We lost the first two games to Washington and Washington State on the road. According to the media, all we needed to do was win our last two games at home against Cal and Stanford—then we would be in good shape for the Big Dance.

We ended up losing to Cal 83-77. The Bears shot lights out and handed us our third loss in the four game stretch.

Hopeless thoughts began to creep past all my resolve.

"Poops, wake up. We're here!" Dee's voice startled me awake.

Trying to open my eyes after the long nap, I looked outside the bus window. It was dark, but lights sparkled on buildings everywhere. "Where are we?" I asked. "This is the *beach*?"

It didn't look like any beach town I had ever imagined.

"No, we're in Las Vegas," Dee said.

"Las Vegas?! What's that?" All I could see were lights and tall buildings everywhere. I was beginning to think I would never get to the beach.

"C'mon, let's go!" Dee said, hurrying me along again. "We have to check in."

I didn't know what was going on. I was sad; this wasn't the beach, I was missing my dad, and none of this seemed right.

But I was seven. I listened to my mother's instructions and followed her into the hotel.

This wasn't the beach trip I had pictured in my mind. I was pretty disappointed.

The loss against Cal was the beginning of the end for me. I was ready for our season to be over. I was hardly playing, and we were losing. I was over it.

Our record was sitting at 18–12, which certainly didn't help our chances of making it into the

Tournament. The only way to plead our case into the Big Dance was simple: *WIN!*

As much as I wanted the season to end, I knew I couldn't fix my mind on that. I went into auto-pilot mode, as if nothing was changing. I wanted to do what was necessary for the good of the team, just as I had always done.

But, inside, I began thinking ahead to my next move.

We had Stanford up next for our last regular-season game. It was Senior Night for me and David Bagga. No lie, it was bittersweet.

I was sad, but with football dangling in the back of my mind, I was also starting to get excited for the next chapter of my life. My collegiate basketball career had opened against Stanford, and now I was ending my last regular season game against them.

It felt like a full circle for me: completion.

We pulled off the win and finished the season 19-12, hopeful that we had solidified a bid into the Big Dance.

After the game, David and I walked to the opposite end of the court to thank our student section—the Zona Zoo. They were cheering loudly for us, chanting, "THANK YOU, SENIORS, *clap, clap, clap-clap-clap,* THANK YOU, SENIORS!" We were both beaming, ear-to-ear.

This was the end, but a new feeling inside me was growing, making me feel like my ride was just beginning. We still had the Pac-10 Tournament in LA and possibly the NCAA Tournament, but nonetheless I felt relieved. I could see the end, and I was ready for whatever God had for me next.

Our win against Stanford gave the team a little momentum going into the Pac-10 Tournament. Every day that week after basketball practice I worked on routes with Billy. I had a pro day coming in April, and I needed as much time as possible to catch up.

I still couldn't believe I was actually doing this.

As Billy and I worked on combine basics as well as the nuances of being a tight end, it still seemed crazy to me! "Fendi Onobun: football player," I chuckled. I would have never thought in a million years I'd be doing something like this.

Senior Night Spring 2009. *Photo courtesy of University of Arizona Athletics*

But it did have a nice ring to it!

In our conference tournament we were seeded fifth, which matched us against our in-state rival, Arizona State, at the fourth seed. In the last two years, the Sun Devils had our number, beating us four straight games.

It was something many Tucsonian basketball fans weren't accustomed to: for the most part Arizona always ran the rivalry. But not this season.

We were desperate for our twentieth win; with it, we'd break our losing streak to ASU and prove we were worthy of a tournament bid.

But from the start of the game, we struggled, mightily. Sophomore James Harden torched us for 27 points, and we couldn't buy a bucket! The Sun Devils beat us for a third time in one season. The pendulum had swung up North, and we were in trouble.

Our Tourney chances felt slim after that loss in the Staples Center, and it gave me a snapshot of my childhood dream, reminding me how it was ending so different from what I had imagined.

Our loss to ASU didn't help our case for a spot in the 65. We were now considered a bubble team. My frustrations were overwhelming, and I was trying my best to stay sane.

We headed back to Tucson that same day, a lot sooner than I had expected. The following day, I was back in the weight room. I had less than two months till the pro day.

Our loss had put me back in town for the *initial* Arizona pro day. Coach Ed asked me if I wanted to participate. I respectfully declined, telling him I wasn't ready for it. I asked if I could come and watch so I would know what to be ready for in April. He told me yes.

That Saturday I got up early and met up with Keith. He got out of the car with a newspaper in his hand. "Look!" he said.

I grabbed the paper and saw an article about the pro day combine taking place that day on campus. There was a heading that read, "Surprise participants."

There was my name in dark bold letters: **6'6"
Forward FENDI ONOBUN**.

I'm not participating today, I reassured myself.

"What's this about?" I asked Keith.

"Beats me," Keith replied.

I didn't know how word had gotten out, considering I was *only* going there to watch, not participate.

Keith and I headed over to the weight room at McKale Center, where the pro day was taking place. My name was definitely on the list of participants. It was awkward, because I was only coming in as a guest.

Fans don't attend games only to find their names listed on the team's starting lineup, do they? I was puzzled. I wasn't participating, nor did I plan to.

I came in wearing jeans and a t-shirt. The environment was crazy though. So many people were there: NFL scouts from almost every team were in the weight room with notepads, stopwatches, and pens. It was intimidating.

The next thing I knew, my name was being called.

"Fen-Dee-On-Nuh-Bun!"

"Oh, shoot! He just called my name!" I said, looking at Keith in confusion. "Should I go?" I asked him

"Yeah," Keith answered.

I was worried; I didn't want the scouts to think I was afraid, but I hadn't known I was listed to *actually* participate. Coach Ed had told me I could come and watch!

Why were they calling my name?!

There was no way I was ready to work out in front of twenty-five-plus NFL scouts.

"Fen-Dee-On-Nuh-Bun! Are you here?"

I walked up to the New York Jets scout in my street clothes. "Here I am, sir! I'm not participating today, just doing measurements, sir. I'm still in basketball season." I told the scout.

"Okay, well, take your shoes off so we can get your height and weight."

I stood in front of the measuring wall with my heels plastered to it and held still for about ten seconds.

"Onobun; Six feet five inches, two hundred and forty-two pounds!" The scout measuring me yelled out.

"Well, you got some size on ya, kid. You sure you don't want to participate?" The Jets scout asked.

"No, sir, I'm still in basketball season." That was my story, and I was sticking to it.

Granted, I felt like the season was over, but hopefully we still had postseason play.

My size was considered an advantage for this football thing. On the basketball court I was considered "undersized" as a power forward, but in football I was "prototypical" as a tight end. It was crazy.

While I was there watching the other participants, I spoke with a few scouts. It turned out that transitioning from the b-ball court to the football field was quite a popular move. Especially for power forwards, who play a more physical position in basketball.

Add the running, agility, catching, and footwork, and the skills transfer pretty well. Guys who've made the switch from the hardwood to the gridiron have been pretty successful.

The popular ones, like Tony Gonzalez and Julius Peppers, loved hoops first, played both in college, stuck with football, and eventually turned it into a profession. They were both drafted.

Antonio Gates made the switch to football his senior year of high school, but only played basketball during his first three years in college. Later he was signed as an undrafted free agent in the NFL and became an instant success.

All I was hearing in the weight room was that scouts were looking for the next "Antonio Gates," the next basketball player who could come in and do what he did.

It sounded like a one-in-a-million chance. But I knew that with the right opportunity there could be a chance. I just needed some direction.

After watching the first pro day, I was able to see what I needed to prepare for in April.

Billy and I had some work to do.

Now that our regular season was over, I wasn't sure if we were going into the NCAA Tourney or not. While we waited to learn our destiny, I began to concentrate more of my time on getting ready for my pro day.

But I still had a foot in the door with hoops: the coaches told us, tournament or not, we would have postseason play.

CHAPTER 4

HOW SWEET IT IS

I remember speaking with our interim head coach Russ Pennell about our chances of making it to the NCAA Tourney. He told me that he honestly did not know. Our assistant coach, Mike Dunlap, said it didn't look good.

Coach Pennell told the media that even if we didn't make it, we'd still play in the National Invitation Tournament—NIT, or Not In Tourney, as we thought of it. It was the tourney for the teams who didn't make the field of 65, the "second fiddle" tournament.

I honestly didn't want to play in the NIT. If that was where we were headed, I was ready to wrap it up.

March 15th finally rolled around. It was Selection Sunday: the one-hour program on CBS that announces the 65 teams that will be dancing in the Tournament. Since the coaches had said we were going to have postseason play regardless, we had an early shoot-around practice that morning.

Afterwards we gathered as a team to watch the program. My junior year we had waited forty-nine minutes before we found out if we had made the tourney, and *that* was stressful.

Now March Madness took on a new meaning. Everyone's nerves were high; you could just feel it.

This year we were in a worse predicament and even more unsure. We had the feeling "We're Arizona, we're always in the tourney… right?" but we were also a bubble team. We didn't know how it was all going to go down.

We had lost our head coach for the second year in a row and had just come through a tumultuous up-and-down season, we weren't sure how it was going play out.

All we could do was wait and see.

Five minutes into the show they started off with the Midwest region, calling the 1 vs. 16 seed first. Louisville had the top seed, and they were playing Morehead State.

After that, they announced the second bracket: 8 vs. 9. Ohio State was playing 9 seed Siena. The third bracket was the 5 vs. 12 game. Utah was announced as the number 5 seed.

"And the Utes will be facing the Arizona Wildcats as a 12th seed," the announcer said.

Oh my God!!!!!!!!!

The entire room went *ballistic!* Everybody screamed, ran, and jumped for joy. It was probably one of the most exciting moments I experienced in my entire career at Arizona.

We really didn't know what our future held in the land of 65. It was such a relief, but a lot of us were surprised. We had hoped to hear our name called, but we also didn't expect it—especially so early.

WOW! God had something special for us. We had gone through so much turmoil and craziness, but this moment made the journey worth it.

I honestly hadn't thought we had a chance. All the smaller conference schools were winning games and creating upsets, and USC won the Pac-10 Tournament to receive an automatic bid: there just didn't seem like a way for us to get in.

But like the saying goes, *God will make a way out of no way!* At that moment, I felt we were supposed to accomplish something special. I didn't know what it was, but I believed it was destined for us.

Now that we had new life for a new season, the staff had to get us prepared for Utah. We were still full of shock, excitement, and relief: we wouldn't be known as the team that broke the Tournament streak. This bid gave Arizona our twenty-fifth consecutive invitation into the Tourney.

I put football on hold to get ready for our second season. It was tourney time, and we were on our way to Miami for the first round of the NCAAs!

We arrived in Miami two days before our game and practiced really well. A lot of the Tourney analysts felt that we did not belong in the Tournament, but there was nothing they could do about it. We were in.

From then on, the big story was: "How is a team that isn't *supposed* to be in the Tournament going to play in the Tournament?" If we did well, we'd prove all the naysayers wrong. If we stunk, well, it would prove all the pundits right.

But like I said before, I felt like we were destined for something special.

We played Utah that Friday night and beat them 84-71 to advance to the second round of the tournament with ease. It was the first time we had advanced since my freshman season.

Our next game was going to be against Cleveland State or Wake Forest. We were anticipating Wake, but Cleveland State took it to the Demon Deacons and beat them in the first round. So our next matchup was against the thirteenth seed Cleveland State Vikings in the second round.

They had two really good players on their team: a combo guard and a forward named J'Nathan Bullock, who was their leading scorer. The coaches said Bullock was about my size: 6'5", 240 lbs., and looked like a football player on the court—sounded familiar. He was Cleveland State's best player.

During practice that week I played as J'Nathan on the scout team. I was the go-to man, and everything went through me. I was killing it! Literally making everything I shot, taking the ball to the rack, blowing by defenders left and right. I couldn't be stopped.

If that wasn't any indication to the coaches that I still had it, then it was for me. That practice alone gave me a feeling I hadn't felt in a while. It reminded that I could play this game at the next level. It gave me peace in my spirit that no matter what happened after Arizona, if I really wanted to pursue a career in hoops, I would be able to.

By game day, our team was ready to go. We started off great, just like we did against Utah. Cleveland State never could catch up. We won the game, and the final score was 71-57.

As the clock was winding down I could hear our fans in the stands yelling "Sweet 16! Sweet 16! Sweet 16!"

Oh, how sweet it was! It was the first time in my career we made it out of the first weekend of the Tournament, and the first time Arizona made it to the Sweet 16 since the 2004–2005 season.

We had already exceeded the expectations of many outsiders, including the media. The best part of it all was that we were the only Pac-10 team left standing out of six!

We had the number one seed Louisville Cardinals

Celebrating with teammate Jordan Hill after defeating Cleveland State in the 2nd Round of the NCAA Tournament, March 2009.
Photo credit: Alan Walsh Arizona Daily Wildcat (2009)

up next the following week at Lucas Oil Stadium, where the Indianapolis Colts play. Indy was only an hour away from Louisville, so it was basically going to be a home game for the Cardinals. It was safe to say they'd have home court advantage. With the tourney down to its final sixteen teams, this meant we would be playing on a bigger stage, with brighter lights and more media coverage.

The Sweet 16 was a big deal. I hadn't seen anything like it before. It was an amazing set up: a special court was built and elevated to the center of the football stadium.

I found it ironic: *Maybe I'll be here playing as a NFL tight end one day.*

Louisville had a great team, with about three or four future pros on their squad. We knew we had our work cut out for us, but we felt we were just as good and just as capable of winning—no matter what seed they were.

We were playing good basketball, and anything can happen in the tourney. Hence the name: March Madness.

With all the football talk surrounding my name at our media session I had a few press writers ask me about it. Jokingly, I asked if there were any Colts' scouts in the building.

The following day, an article ran: *"Onobun Thinks Coltish."* Once word got out that I could possibly be making the switch from the hardwood to the gridiron, people started asking me if I was seriously considering it. I was, I just didn't anticipate that a whole article would be written about it.

While I was entertained by the football attention, we still had a game to play. Louisville played a game very similar to ours: run-and-gun and up-tempo. The only difference, and maybe the biggest difference, was their size and depth. This game was going to be a track meet.

Game day had finally come. These were the biggest and brightest lights I had ever played under. Louisville came out on a mission. From the beginning they used their speed, size, and depth, and we couldn't keep up.

The crowd of 33,000+ was filled with Cardinal red, and it basically carried their momentum throughout the entire game. We didn't get off to a good start. They took advantage and never looked back.

Louisville smashed us 103-64, and our season was over just like that. It was Arizona's worst loss in tournament history.

The ride to the Sweet 16 had been fun, but it hurt finishing my career like that.

After the game, I just sat in the locker room, thinking. I had thought a lot about my future, but the realization that it was suddenly here hit quickly. I was done with basketball at Arizona.

Now I had to figure out a plan, because this football thing wasn't guaranteed.

Dee and I walked up to the hotel doors, and I looked up to read the lit-up sign.

EXCALIBUR.

It was a huge white castle of a building, full of games, machines, and tables. Grownups were everywhere, and it was so loud and full of smoke.

I didn't want to be here. I had to figure out how to get away. But how?

I knew my phone number. I had memorized it when I started school so I could call home if I needed. Now, I recited it to myself over and over again: *495-5353, 495-5353, 495-5353.*

I needed a plan. I needed a way to get out. I felt stuck, and I was so sad Dee hadn't brought me to the beach.

"Dee, where's the beach over here?" I kept asking. "Where's the beach?!"

"We have to go to the room, Poops! Let's go!" was the only answer I got.

I dragged my feet across the hall before we entered the elevator. I just stood there, arms folded and sad. But I was thinking of a plan. A plan to get to a phone, so I could call my dad. I wanted to go home.

CHAPTER **5**

A NEW ROAD

My collegiate season was officially over. I was at a crossroads.

I told myself, "Basketball is my first love, my dream sport; I really want to pursue it professionally." But I just didn't know how to go about it.

The season had been over a few days, and I hadn't heard from an agent, or anyone for that matter. I was anxious to find an opportunity; I just had to figure out how.

I still had a pro day in April, and I had to make sure I was ready for that. But I didn't know where that was going to take me either. By taking only one class, I was able to focus on football training while playing basketball to keep in shape.

It was a weird time; I was double training. Every single day, I was doing things for football during the day

with Billy, and then I would turn around and do basketball workouts at night.

I started wondering why was I working at basketball
when I wasn't even sure of any future basketball opportunities. I knew the answer: It was because of my *love*
for the game.

My career hadn't gone as planned at Arizona, but I
knew if an opportunity presented itself I was going to
take it, and I would be ready.

And as for football, I wasn't sure if I was doing the
right thing by pursuing a sport I barely knew anything
about; but I'm a big believer in doors being opened by
God. If God opens a door, you walk through it. That
was my mantra.

Another person who kept my spirits up during my
last two years at Arizona was Jon Demeter, JD, my spiri-
tual mentor and friend. JD kept me motivated and encouraged through the rough time and always reminded me to not worry: the Lord had a great plan for me,
no matter what it was.

JD was part of Athletes In Action (AIA)—a world-
wide sports ministry that teaches athletes a way to
merge God and sport and apply those lessons to life.
He was the campus director at Arizona, and we often
talked about what I should pursue.

An opportunity came up through AIA to play in a
basketball round robin for two weeks in Poland. There
was also an opportunity to serve and share my faith with
the people of Poland while I was there as well. It sounded like an amazing opportunity, and I definitely wanted
to take advantage of it. I completed all the paperwork
and talked with the right people to get everything set
up. Then I realized there was a schedule conflict.

My pro day was during the second week of the tour. There was no way I could do it.

Billy said it was normal for guys to be called days after their pro day or days before the draft to come and workout.

My heart wanted to hoop, and it would have been cool to experience the trip, but Keith and Billy and I knew the football opportunity was too slim to miss. If there was any hope of it working out, I couldn't miss the pro day.

I believed that more basketball opportunities would present themselves, but I wasn't sure if there would be any more for football. I wanted to make sure my schedule was clear, just in case I did get a call for a workout or an invitation to camp.

April was near, and I could feel my attention shifting more towards football. I was still working on my hoops, but I was more focused on my pro day. I worked every day with Billy on 40-yard dash starts, routes, and drills.

My basketball strength coach, Jimmy Krumpos, helped me train for the 225 bench press test. More than ever, I was committed to this football thing. I wanted to make sure that, come April, I was fully prepared.

I knew it was going to be huge opportunity: freaking NFL scouts were going to be there!

Keith was really good friends with one of the football coaches at Arizona. He heard about me giving football a shot and asked Keith if I would be interested in playing for the Wildcat football team as a fifth-year senior.

When Keith relayed the question to me, I realized that at this point I wanted to move on from Arizona. Maybe I was bitter after my basketball career, but mainly

I just wanted a change. I didn't want to be in Tucson anymore, and I didn't want to spend a fifth year at UA.

The initial plan Keith, Billy, and I came up with was this: kill my pro day, get a phone call, try out, and then make an NFL practice squad.

A little much? No way! Why not shoot for the top?

That was my plan, and I was sticking to it. I dedicated everything to this NFL thing. Word got out fast, and everybody knew what I was doing.

I still wasn't completely sure if I was doing the right thing, or if football was really something God wanted me to do. But I felt that He had presented the opportunity, so I was going to give it a shot.

There were some other notable Division I basketball players thinking about making the same transition, so the idea was gaining some popularity. A point guard out of Duke was trying to make the transition to quarterback, and Cleveland State's J'Nathan Bullock—the guy we had just played against in the Tourney—was also trying to become a tight end.

Goodbye Basketball. Hello Football? Spring 2009. *Photo credit: Alan Walsh Arizona Daily Wildcat (2009)*

Days were passing by quickly, and April was near. I knew that we had just cobbled together a training program, but we did the best we could with the time and resources available.

I was going to take the little bit of training I had and use my athleticism to the best of my ability. I was all in, and it was now or never.

I was trying to go pro.

CHAPTER 6

TRYNA'
GO PRO

It was a Saturday morning, April 11th. The time had finally come. My pro day was finally here. It was a rainy and muggy day—a rarity in Tucson.

I was worried I wasn't going to be able to run routes in front of the scouts; nevertheless, I was excited, anxious, and—more than anything—I was ready.

I got to the McKale Center weight room two hours early so I could get prepared for the workout. I was in a zone. I was going to put everything I had learned to use today. The Lord was with me, and I was confident that this was the beginning of my NFL career.

As the other two Arizona football players and I were warming up with Coach Ed, the scouts began to trickle in. The Carolina Panthers, the Buffalo Bills, and the New England Patriots were in attendance. A few of my basketball teammates came out to watch as well. And, of course, Keith and Billy were in the gym, watching my big day.

They looked like two proud uncles watching their nephew warm up for his first little league game.

This was the day I had been waiting for, and it was finally here. I knew my athleticism would carry me through on a few drills. I wasn't too concerned about the 40-yard dash, the standing vertical, and the broad jump.

What I was concerned about were the L drill and the shuttle run; I wasn't too familiar with those drills. I had looked up a few techniques on YouTube, and that was it. I was just going to wing that part and put the outcome in God's hands.

No matter what happened, I was ready, and it was time.

The first drill was the 40-yard dash. This was probably the most important drill of them all. Speed kills, so I wanted to make sure I killed it. From the little training I had done with Billy, I was consistently running 4.5s and some 4.4s—really fast for a guy my size. I was pretty confident about this one.

Right before I took the line, I said a quick prayer, set myself up, and *took off*!

It felt great! I was *blazing*! Billy clocked it and hand signaled to me 4.44; however, the scouts said they weren't ready, and I needed to rerun it.

"What?!" I yelled in disbelief. I couldn't believe it.

After the first two guys ran their 40-yard dash, I re-did mine. This time I made sure the scouts were ready. Once I took the line I said a quick prayer again, set myself up, paused for a few seconds then *took off*. Again. When I ran the second time, I made sure I did it as hard and as fast as I possibly could.

Billy's eyes widened as he signaled 4.48 to me, but the scouts had me at 4.51—still not bad.

I had one more run, since the first one didn't count. I was a little winded, so they gave me some time to catch my breath. After a few moments, I toed the line again and ran my last 40—running with all my might for a third time.

The Panthers' scout clocked me in at 4.50. It had felt slower than the last one, but I had actually shaved some time so I was satisfied.

As I was walking back, I could hear whispers in the crowd; people were surprised at how fast I ran. I found out later that on a national scale my 40 time would have tied for first place out of all the tight ends in the 2009 NFL Combine that had happened the month before.

I was off to a good start.

The next drill up was the standing vertical. I was expecting to jump 35 or 36 inches. I knew I would do well in this drill just from basketball. After my standing reach was measured I was given the OK to jump.

I cleared 35 inches on my first jump easily. I knew I could get a little higher on my second jump. On my second go-round, I cleared 2.5 more inches. I finished with a 37 ½" vertical. I was feeling pretty good.

The scouts moved us to the next drill, which was the "L" drill. After that was the 20-yard shuttle run. I wasn't really familiar with the technique for these two drills, but I gave them a shot. Coach Ed had told me that all the scouts really wanted to see was if I could run and catch a ball.

It felt awkward moving laterally from a three-point stance. I was so used to being upright from hoops. I was happy when those two drills were over. I clocked in at

4.48 seconds on the short shuttle, which was decent, and my "L" drill time would have placed eleventh out of fourteen at the combine.

After the agility drills, we had the broad jump, another athletic jumping drill. It was very similar to the vertical jump, only I was jumping out forward instead of up. My long legs were going to be helpful in this one. I jumped 10'5" for my first jump. My second attempt was 10'7". When I landed, I saw the Patriots' scout nod his head in approval, or maybe he was just surprised. Either way, the combine broad jump record for a tight end that year was 10'3." My jump would have taken first place.

I wrapped up all the field drills, and the position drills were next. With only three of us participating, it didn't take long. I was excited because I had been working really hard on my pass-catching skills. I was ready to show these scouts I could catch.

Since it was raining, we couldn't go outside. One of the scouts improvised and had me stand in different positions while he threw the ball. He had me catching at different angles, just the way Billy and I had worked on it. It couldn't have worked out any better.

I knew I still had some work to do on my route running skills, so maybe the rain that day was a gift from above. The scout threw about thirty balls to me. I only had trouble catching over my right shoulder, but catching twenty-seven of thirty proved I could catch.

After that, we were done. It wasn't as taxing as I thought it would be, but I had given the pro day all I had.

The Patriots' scout told me I had a good workout; I agreed, but I was still nervous to see what was going to happen next. The draft was still a couple of weeks away.

All I could do was sit and wait. I was so excited I didn't know what to do with myself. I couldn't believe I had just created an opportunity to possibly make it to the NFL. I literally could not believe it!

Keith told me that my numbers were amazing; I just needed to get them out to the scouts who weren't present. With the draft just two weeks away and no agent working on my behalf, I made a spreadsheet of my pro day numbers.

I didn't have a way to send it to every NFL scout, so my plan was to send them to all the scouts who usually scouted UA. Kelly Hooker, the assistant administrator at the football office, was very helpful in sending out my information to all the scouts she knew. I also had a pretty good connection with the local newspaper, so I was hoping to get my pro day story some buzz as a reported article.

I contacted J'Nathan Bullock through Facebook to see how his pro transition was going. He told me there were about eighteen scouts at his pro day. He also said the coaches were pretty tough on him—almost as if they didn't want him to succeed. He had an agent working for him as well; that was a huge plus.

I had to find a way to get more buzz; I needed to bring attention to myself quickly. My numbers in a few of the drills were great.

"You can't teach a 6'6" 250-pounder how to run a 40 in 4.5," Keith said.

With a week left before the draft, there was an article written about me on the Buffalo Bills website: "Bills looking at TE sleeper." The article mentioned my pro day stats and said I could be a seventh-round steal.

Seeing that article made me think I might just have a shot at the NFL. It was pretty awesome to read, but I wasn't going to believe the hype until I got a call.

The next day Keith and I created a new package and, thanks to our friend Kelly at the Arizona football office, e-mailed the Bills story to every NFL scout who covered the southwest region. A few scouts replied immediately, wanting to know if I had any film from the pro day workout.

We were glad we received immediate responses, but there was one huge problem: No one had taped my pro day. The scouts wanted to see something, and I had nothing to show them. It wasn't like I had played football this past season. I really had to improvise.

A few days before I had just finished making a highlight tape of my basketball career and I was sending it off to European basketball agents. My hoops film wouldn't help me get to the gridiron, but I had a friend in the media arts department who was willing to make a cut-up of me for football as well. The timing couldn't have been better.

We brainstormed some ideas and got rolling. I needed something fast. With the draft only six days away, we were able to film a workout of me catching footballs and running routes. Billy played quarterback and worked me through the tight end route tree.

I was able to get the film cut and edited to DVD form in about two days. Time was running out; the draft was in four days. I had to get my video out fast!

Afterwards, I got it posted on YouTube. It was amazing considering the time constraints. I *finally* had something to show the scouts—it wasn't my pro day, nor was it game footage, but it was something to see. I was hoping this video would be my ticket to the NFL.

I couldn't get the link out fast enough! We contacted the thirteen teams that replied requesting film. I forwarded the link to the football secretary right away, and she forwarded it to the scouts.

Just three days remained before the draft, so I was definitely pushing it. All I could do was hope for the best.

Once the link was sent, we were told that no scouts had yet replied. But the video had one hundred hits the first day it was up. The next day, we still hadn't heard anything, but the hits went up another fifty. We were two days away from the draft.

I was getting worried, and nobody was saying anything. I had done all I could to this point. I even wrote a follow-up email for Kelly to send on my behalf.

Was it too late?

Dee and I walked into a box of a room at the hotel. "We're here! We're on vacation now!"

I looked around at the four walls. She had told me we were going to the beach. "Why are we here?" I asked.

"I changed the vacation. It's going to be fun!"

I looked around again. There was nothing for me to do. I could see all the sparkling lights outside, but they just made me miss Houston. *What are we doing here?*

The next morning, I woke up early to go to the restroom. I didn't know what time it was, but I knew it was early. There was a telephone in the bathroom. I wasn't sure if my dad was up, but I picked up the telephone in the bathroom and tried to dial him at home.

I recited my home number in my head and gently pressed the numbers 4, 9, 5, 5, 3, 5, 3.

There was an automated response. I hung up and tried again. 495-5353… nothing. Same response. I couldn't get through, and I didn't know why. My number had always worked before, and I didn't know why it wasn't working now.

I tried one last time. I just wanted to talk to my dad and go home.

I dialed the number more slowly, hoping it would go through.

I couldn't get to him. I hung the phone up and sighed as my chin sunk to my chest. I was out of options. If I couldn't call him, how I was going to get a hold of my dad? I had tried the only thing a seven-year-old knew to do.

I just had to wait and hope I'd get to go back home and see my dad again. It was clear I wasn't going to the beach. And I wasn't a fan of the changed vacation.

Everything seemed wrong.

The draft was a day away. There was nothing more I could do other than hope the right person had seen that video. It sounded ridiculous, but I believed I had a chance.

I had exhausted all my options to this point. I didn't know how this thing was going to play out.

It was time to play the waiting game.

CHAPTER **7**

DREAM DEFERRED

April 25, 2009, the day of the NFL Draft. I knew a couple of guys who were expecting to hear their name called so I watched it—for the first time in my life!

It was pretty lengthy. I didn't have a draft party or anything outlandish like that, but I *did* keep a close eye on it in the later rounds from my Tucson apartment.

Two guys on our football team ended up getting drafted by the Jacksonville Jaguars. Our starting tackle was picked up in the second round, and UA's top wide receiver was snatched in the fourth. I had hoped to hear my name somewhere in the seventh round, like that article had mentioned.

When the draft was over, my name hadn't been called.

I understood that I was new to this football thing, but I was disappointed. I shouldn't have been, but I was really hoping to get a call, even if it was just for a tryout. But that didn't happen either.

The draft was over, and priority undrafted free agents were getting picked up. Maybe it had been a little crazy of me to think I would actually get drafted into the NFL with no playing experience. Maybe that was a ridiculous thought.

But why had scouts been looking at me?

Arizona's starting linebacker signed as an undrafted free agent to the Redskins. A friend of mine from Texas A&M was signed by the Seahawks after the draft as well. J'Nathan from Cleveland State got picked by the Jets! Why wasn't I getting any calls?

I called Billy. He reassured me that undrafted free agents don't *always* get a call right after the draft; some don't receive a call until maybe two or three days later.

I remained hopeful, but I still didn't hear anything. Every time my phone rang I looked to see if it was from an unknown area code, expecting it to be a coach or scout. If it wasn't, I didn't even bother to pick up. Unfortunately, the only calls I did receive from unknown area codes were from annoying telemarketers, which did nothing but add to the anger that was rising within me.

My thoughts were running wild. *Was football my sport? No! Had I played the sport? Not since middle school! But I pushed hoops to the backburner for this. Was it just a waste of time?*

I knew I couldn't compare my journey to those who had put their lives into football with dreams of making it to the NFL, but I was definitely riding this football wave. I thought I legitimately had a shot.

Then I reminded myself that our star quarterback hadn't even gotten a call. My feelings didn't compare to those of others like him, but I was still mad. I had just *known* I would at *least* get a look.

Was this a sign? Maybe God didn't want me to do this football thing. Or maybe it was a test to see how much I really loved basketball. I had no idea.

Four days had passed after the draft, and I knew I wasn't getting a call—my phone didn't ring at all. It was frustrating.

Was it because I hadn't played since middle school? Was it because I didn't have game film? Maybe I needed an agent.

The point was, I had no clue; but I wanted answers and wanted them now!

I felt a guy with my size and athleticism should have at least gotten a look, a tryout… *something*! Overzealous? Maybe. But I was in disbelief.

I couldn't lie: I may have said that I didn't, but I had bought into my hype—especially after the article on the Bills' website. Keith called the scouts who were at my pro day to get some answers. Those were the people we needed to question; they had seen me!

All three scouts gave him their brief analysis.

The Patriots' scout thought I was good enough and had a chance to make a practice squad, but their team was full of tight ends at the time. The Panthers felt my initial burst off the line was too slow, and I wasn't a Carolina Panther type of tight end—whatever that meant.

The Bills' scout stated that I was good and had potential, but their team did not have the time or the resources to teach the game at its highest level to someone who had never played. That made sense. He suggested to Keith that I try NFL Europe or an arena league. He told him that something like that would help me gain more experience.

NFL Europe no longer existed, and the arena league was nowhere near the talent level of the NFL. Not to mention the arena league was faltering, so those weren't useful options at all.

I had decided when I started this thing that if I was going to play football, I wanted to go to the league. Period.

After speaking to the scouts, they referred us to other scouts, assuming they'd be interested. We had numbers from San Diego to Philadelphia, but as we began to make calls, the situation was the same. One scout would refer us to another scout, who would refer us to another scout, and so on.

No team had a need for a guy who hadn't played football since middle school. Who was I kidding? If this was the case, I might as well have given the MLB a shot, too.

This was the time; teams had already signed their free agents. Keith called the scouts of teams that were close to us—Arizona, San Diego, and Denver—hoping they'd give me a chance. No luck.

It was rough, but Keith kept trying. He reached out to a scout from the Seattle Seahawks; surprisingly, the scout knew who I was. *Yes, he had actually heard of me!* It shocked Keith, because the other fifteen scouts he spoke to hadn't.

Keith told me Seattle already had my name on their list for a tryout. There wasn't an exact date for it, but the scout told him it would be sometime after the NBA Draft in July, before their training camp. It was a one-to-three-day minicamp.

I was definitely excited for the tryout. It was *another* shot at the NFL! That call boosted my spirits so much, and it stopped me from thinking I was wasting my time with this football stuff.

With this tryout in the immediate future, I started working out with the Arizona football team. I wanted to be—no, I *had* to be—ready for this tryout. I knew it was nearly three months away, but that gave me more time to get better.

I played 7-on-7 with the team and ran routes for the quarterbacks. It was such a different atmosphere being with them.

For starters, I wasn't indoors shooting jump shots, dunking or playing H-O-R-S-E. I was outside with cleats and gloves and I was running tight end routes on the field. Some of the guys had given me some pointers while I was out there with them. It was pretty cool, and I actually felt like I was on the squad.

Since I hadn't gotten a call after the draft, I had signed up to play in a basketball showcase in Las Vegas. International pro basketball scouts would be in attendance, seeking talent in the States. It sounded like a good opportunity and a segue to the start of a pro basketball career. I committed to play in Vegas since I hadn't heard anything from the football side. But now I had this Seahawks tryout. I was worried about the dates of both events clashing.

The Vegas opportunity had a date and was something concrete. This tryout for Seattle sounded good, but the scout wasn't too definitive on a date, so I wasn't sure if it was going to happen or not. I couldn't decide which direction I wanted to go.

Not to mention Keith was in my ear about another suggestion that had been made by some of the scouts he had spoken to: Go back to school for a fifth year and *play* college football.

Keith believed it was the next best option. It made sense, especially if I was trying to make it to the NFL. But for me it was pro or nothing, whichever way that meant, football or basketball.

"Fendi, you should play for the football team here," he said. "That would be amazing! You and Gronk, oh my goodness!"

Our starting tight end was Rob Gronkowski, probably the team's best player, coming off his sophomore season. Keith really wanted me to consider playing football in Tucson; but I was about to receive my bachelor's degree, and I didn't want to go back to school for another year. My four years at UA had been rough, and I really just wanted to move forward.

I did have a year of eligibility left. Each student-athlete gets five total years of eligibility. In most cases, if the fifth year is used, it's for a redshirt season—which I almost burned through my freshman year. Since my redshirt was pulled, I had an extra year available. The catch is you can only have four non-redshirt seasons in one sport, and I used those in basketball.

However, I could use my fifth year in another sport, in this case football.

Regardless of the rule, I still didn't want to do another year of school. But I did want to keep pursuing football.

The curiosity of wondering if I could really play this game at the next level developed a hunger in me to keep pushing. I wanted to keep trying, and I wasn't satisfied with stopping.

I didn't get a call and that motivated me more; yet I didn't have a date for my Seattle workout, and no other pro teams were looking at me. How in the world was I supposed to get to the NFL?

"Just go to school, Fendi. Just one year. I guarantee it will help you." Keith said.

"No!" I told him. "I'm done with school. I've earned my degree."

I didn't want to play football at Arizona, and he knew that from day one. My mind hadn't changed. I didn't have anything against the Wildcats; I just didn't want to spend another year in school there.

My dad got involved, and he thought it was the best plan too—as far as football was concerned—but I really wanted to get to the next part of my life. Graduation was less than a week away, and I was ready to move on.

Despite my protests, Keith and my dad continued to push one more year of school. I didn't care how frustrated either of them was with my decision. I was about to receive my college degree and graduate.

It was an exciting time for me. I put what I was calling this "football stuff" on hold and focused on my amazing accomplishment. It was good to have my family and loved ones celebrate my seventeen years of education. Receiving my college degree was something that had always been important to me; now it was coming to pass, and I was very proud of myself, as was my family.

Graduation Day! May 2009.
Photo courtesy of University of Arizona Athletics

Once graduation was over, all the back and forth between myself, dad, and Keith pushed me away from the football plan. I got back to working in the gym, back to ball handling drills, jump shots, and basketball conditioning for this showcase in Las Vegas. I needed to get ready if I was going to be playing in front of international scouts.

I could no longer think of a good reason to focus my energy on a sport I hadn't played since middle school. I had wasted my time with all of the NFL training, and I just wanted to go back to what I knew I could do.

Once I decided to continue pursuing basketball, my spirit felt peaceful. I wasn't sure how real my Seahawks tryout was, anyway. And it had finally dawned on me that making it to the NFL through a mini camp would be unlikely.

CHAPTER 8

CROSSROADS

I was a college graduate with the world at my fingertips. This was the moment I had been waiting for. The time I had been rushing to reach. What came next?

Who knew?

My dad wanted to know what was next and I honestly didn't know. I was torn between two sports I wanted to pursue, and I was in a predicament.

I was shaky on the NFL because nothing seemed certain, but Dad didn't like the idea of me playing pro basketball overseas. Keith wouldn't accept "no" for an answer, and he kept trying to convince me to stay and play football in Tucson for another year. It was literally madness.

Earlier during graduation week, my dad and I had met Keith for lunch. I knew the football talk would come back up. I couldn't believe how much they were trying to convince me to stay and play.

Keith said, "You could just use the time to learn the game. Watch how it's played; get some film. Improve your skills from practice. It would be great to learn from Rob and gain some experience."

Yeah, the idea sounded good, but bump that—I wasn't for it. Call me crazy, but I wasn't receptive to the idea at all. I felt like I had watched for four years on the basketball team. I didn't want to watch anymore.

"What do you think you'd be doing on a NFL practice squad?" Keith asked.

It was a good question. "I'd be getting paid!" I responded with a laugh. "I'd be getting paid to watch, learn, and practice!"

Keith smirked. "The point is you'd be watching, Fendi. But you can't get there from where you are now. You need more experience, and playing college football here is the perfect way to get it."

As much as Keith and my dad had pressed me to play, and as much as I pushed back against them, in my heart, I had often contemplated suiting up for the Wildcats football team—especially when I was out there running routes with the guys. But by this point, I knew I wasn't even going to entertain it.

I had so much other stuff on my mind that week, and all the talk from them was only making it worse. I was sick of this football chase, and I didn't want to deal with it anymore.

I felt like God was pretty clear about what I should be doing. I saw the signs. I had tried the NFL thing, and it just wasn't working. I didn't think football was in His plans for me. I was going to get ready for this basketball showcase and see where it led.

The week was bittersweet. After graduation, Keith wanted me to meet with his friend who was the director of player operations for the school's football team. I had about ten days left in Tucson before I left for Phoenix to train for the basketball showcase. I didn't know why Keith wanted me to meet his friend. I told him several times I wasn't interested in playing.

"Just see if they can help you out. Maybe they have a scholarship or something," Keith said.

"Keith, really? I don't want to play here, man! I'm tired of this football foolishness; it's stupid!"

"Fendi, just do it for me, please. It doesn't hurt to sit and talk to someone. He's cool! Just talk to him." Keith was so persistent.

I remember just looking at him annoyed and shaking my head because he wouldn't let it go.

"If you promise to leave me alone about this, Keith, I'll do it."

"Deal!" he said with a smile.

The next afternoon, Wednesday afternoon, I walked into the Arizona football office to see Keith's friend Coach Harp. I was a little nervous. There were a few people waiting in the lobby, but the first person I saw was Keith, with the biggest smile on his face.

"Fendi, I'm glad you were able to stop by!"

I looked at him with the hardest sarcastic smirk ever. "Ummm-hmmm," I replied.

"Hey Fendi!" It was Megan Seymour, Billy's wife. She worked with Keith, and she was another fan of the idea of me playing football for Arizona. It didn't surprise me to see her there either.

"Hey, Meg," I replied.

Coach Harp, a few other people, and another football coach were all in the lobby, too. Something just didn't seem right. I thought I was just going to meet with Harp.

Was this a setup?

"Coach Stoops should be out of his meeting in a few," said Coach Harp when I shook his hand.

"Wait! What did you say?" I questioned Harp.

"Stoops," Harp said.

I turned to Keith. "Coach Stoops? You set up a meeting with Coach Stoops for me?"

"Well, I just wanted you to talk to him. Maybe he could help you out," Keith responded.

I couldn't believe he had set me up like this. I was livid. "I knew this was a setup! You told me to come meet with Harp; you said nothing about Stoops!"

"Fen, just see what he has to say. What can it hurt?" said Megan.

I was so mad. I didn't want to play football here, nor did I want to waste Coach Stoops' time. And here I was about to have a meeting with him, the head football coach.

We all sat there and waited, but Coach Stoops never made it around to meet me. I did talk with Harp in his office, though. He told me the football team had no scholarships available; they were actually one man over.

"If you want to come out on your own expense, though, you're more than welcome to join us."

There was no way I was going to pay for school on my own. Especially after just completing my college education for free! My last four years of school were paid for through my basketball scholarship, and I wasn't going to spend a dime on school just to chase some misguided dream.

Then Harp's assistant director told me if I *did* come out and join the team, I probably wouldn't play very much. But he assured me I'd "gain some experience."

I left the office that day with so much clarity.

Committing myself to the pro day and having nothing happen draft-wise should have been the first sign for me. I understood that being drafted was somewhat of a stretch, but there was still the possibility of a phone call. That didn't even happen. Now the whole UA football option—although it had never been an option for me to begin with—had no scholarships available. And I hadn't heard from anyone with the Seahawks in months.

Coach Harper suggested I set up a one-on-one with Coach Stoops, adding that maybe he could help me with some alternative options, schools that had football scholarships available through *his* connections. Maybe Coach Stoops *could* help me find another school—possibly a school at home in Houston.

I was fed up with the football shenanigans, but I realized it wouldn't hurt to see what options he might have. I had done everything else. I scheduled a meeting with Coach Stoops for Monday morning the following week.

I felt God was very clear with what I had been facing. No matter how many ways I tried to approach football, it just wasn't working. There were others, though, who believed it was the right direction for me and felt I was going to find a place to play football.

My Vegas basketball showcase was coming up in July, and I was really looking forward to that. My passion for hoops was coming back, and it felt good. The basketball jones was flowing through me again, and I was in the gym working on my game every night.

I was pretty sure I was going to give the football thing up for good. Seattle was falling further and further from my mind, and the timing of the tryout didn't make much sense to me.

Once my family left Tucson after graduation, I wanted to take some time and clear my thoughts. I needed to think about what I wanted to do with my future—by myself—and now was a good time to do so. I had just a few more days in Tucson.

I was still thinking about the possibility of a pro career overseas. I knew the economy was in a bad state, and the amount of money I would likely be offered for my first contract wouldn't be much. The basketball agent had told me I'd make anywhere from \$35,000 to \$40,000 my first year, and I began wondering whether it was worth leaving everything I knew for that amount of money.

Many overseas teams recruit Americans who can instantly help their teams. I knew I had that ability, but I was just going to have to work my way up. I wasn't going to see six figures coming out of college. At best, until I proved myself, I wouldn't earn more than \$50,000 or so—*if* things went well for me.

It wasn't a bad amount of tax-free money, but that was a *best-case scenario*. Yet, there was the uncertainty of being paid, teams going bankrupt, and the lifestyle overseas. It was all in question for me.

With time to myself now, I wrote down a list of opportunities I had coming out of school as a college graduate. Outside of sports, I wanted to work in the marketing department of a big time shoe corporation such as Nike™. It was something I had been considering if things didn't shake up for me athletically.

I had also done an internship with the Phoenix Suns the previous summer. I was coming off leg surgery and couldn't do any basketball training, so I used the down time to learn the business side of the NBA. Coach Olson got me connected, and I shadowed some of the operations staff during my class internship there.

I was able to build a good relationship with the Suns' senior VP, David Griffin, and the general manager, Steve Kerr, an Arizona basketball legend. I had aspirations of one day working within the operational side of an NBA franchise, and the internship revealed I had an even greater interest for it than I had imagined.

Another option I considered was getting more involved with Athletes in Action sports ministry. Becoming an active member on campus had really changed my life as I grew closer to the ministry. My relationship with JD was great, and it was another thing I saw myself doing—I just wasn't sure if I wanted to do it now.

So I had a few options and different directions I could go, I just didn't know what to do or what I really wanted to do. The alone time was good. I wanted to make a decision for me, not a decision for everyone else.

I still had a meeting to follow up with Coach Stoops. I was praying and praying that God's will would be done in that meeting with him. I wasn't sure how Coach Stoops could help me if he had no scholarships left to give, but it didn't hurt to hear what he had to say.

I wasn't obligated to do anything.

CHAPTER **9**

DECISIONS...
DECISIONS

A friend of JD's, whom I knew pretty well, was a guy by the name of Doug Gotcher, aka Gotch (Goe-tch). He was the national director of Athletes in Action, and I was pretty cool with him from my involvement in AIA. He told me if I ever needed help with basketball or football to reach out to him. So I did.

I told Gotch how I felt uncertain about pro basketball overseas and how the opportunities presented to me weren't very appealing. Since he was coming from the outside, I felt he could give me sound advice without any bias.

Gotch truly understood how I felt and was aware of the roller coaster career I had on the hardwood. Once I voiced to him why I *didn't* want to be at Arizona any longer he didn't push me to stay and try football.

I told him that if I *was* going to go back to school, I had realized that I wanted to go back to Houston—my hometown. I told him that a change of scenery while doing something different would be ideal. Plus, I'd be home with my family.

I asked Gotch if he wouldn't mind contacting Rice University and talking to their football recruiting coordinator about me. I forwarded to him the YouTube link that I created for the NFL scouts. Gotch found the contact information, called Rice's coordinator and spoke to him about me, then sent my YouTube link via email.

Nobody knew I was even considering this move. I hadn't talked much to Keith after he set up that meeting, and things were a little awkward between my dad and I because he wasn't very happy about me pursuing pro basketball overseas.

I asked Gotch to help me because I knew he wouldn't force anything. He just wanted to help me anyway he could.

Gotch said that once the recruiting coordinator received the link, he watched it and called him right back. They were definitely interested. I had to fax over some paperwork, and within a few minutes they had it. Rice was a challenging academic private school in Houston, but my grades were good enough to get in. I didn't think it would be a problem to get accepted.

I also did more research and saw they had just lost their starting tight end James Casey to the NFL draft. He had led the Rice Owls in receptions and touchdowns this past season. It felt like a good fit. I would be back at home doing something I decided to do—not something someone else decided for me.

Once all my paperwork was in, I had to play the waiting game for a bit. I wasn't allowed to talk to Rice's recruiting coordinator due to NCAA regulations, so Gotch kept me in the loop.

By the end of the week the coordinator from Rice finally responded. He told Gotch it was going to be tough to get me in.

I spoke with our compliance guy at UA to see why my request for transfer didn't go through. Based on the rules, I couldn't transfer into another school as an undergrad, only as a graduate student. I wasn't a grad student.

There were so many complications involved with transferring to Rice that it just didn't make sense to pursue it.

A*nother* football attempt shut down. At this point I felt stupid. No matter how much I tried, this football thing wasn't working. I thought Rice was the perfect fit, especially after they had just lost their starting tight end to the Houston Texans.

But that's all it was: a *thought.*

I was continuously running into dead ends, and they just gave me more reason to believe that football wasn't the path for me. I began to think of how many ways God could show me.

I thought I was doing the right thing, but I broke down. I had never felt like I forced an issue *so* much, only to fail over and over again. The message was clear: I had to let it go. I felt it in my heart that football just wasn't my route. God had something different for me.

He had to.

After I found out about Rice, I really didn't want to go see Coach Stoops. Rice was a no-go, and I wasn't going to play for Arizona.

I saw two doors in front of me. One door was the Seahawks tryout that I still didn't know much about. The second door was the Vegas Showcase. Those were my only options if I wanted to be a professional athlete.

At that point, I finally decided to just let go and let God.

I was no longer going to force anything, but instead I would let things come as they may. No matter what Coach Stoops had to say, I already had my options lined up. I was going to pursue what was presented and let God take care of the rest.

That Monday morning, I went to the football office. I got there a little early, so I sat in the car and waited until it was time.

I was checking my email when I saw something in my inbox from Coach Stoops' secretary titled "Meeting with Coach Stoops." I opened it, and it read:

Fendi,

Coach Stoops will not be able to meet with you this morning and will have to re-schedule.

Sorry for the inconvenience.

I couldn't believe it. I read it again to make sure I had read her email correctly. Another failed attempt. If that wasn't a sign right there, I didn't know what was!

The coach's cancellation gave me more assurance about the situation. I didn't even bother to respond to the email or make a third attempt to reschedule. It was clear to me. I had to listen to God. I knew He would direct my path; and I really had to stop forcing everything.

I wasn't even upset that Coach Stoops had canceled our appointment. I was OK with it, because I believed it was an affirmation that what was going to happen was already ordained to happen. Now I could just focus on getting ready for the showcase and the tryout I supposedly had with the Seahawks.

Later that day I went to McKale Center to pick up some empty boxes that were left out for me to pack up my Tucson apartment. Just as I was approaching the boxes by the entrance door, Coach Stoops came jogging towards me. I couldn't tell if he was in a rush to get somewhere or just on his afternoon jog.

Oh, shoot. My eyes widened.

I looked at him and gave a cordial nod to say hello.

He responded and waved. "Hey, weren't we supposed to meet today?"

"Yeah, at 10:00 this morning," I said. It was now 1:00 in the afternoon.

"Give me fifteen minutes, and let's meet up," he said.

"Alright," I heard myself saying.

What the...? Was this a test to see if I had really let this football stuff go?

"God, what do you want me to do?" I asked. I was so confused now.

I went by the entrance door to grab the boxes and waited in the car until I saw Coach Stoops come back. I already knew the team didn't have any scholarships, so I wondered what he was going to say. It didn't really matter anyway. I knew I had a plan.

We met back up in front of the football office. We talked for a little bit, and then he asked how the situation with Rice was going.

I was surprised, because I didn't know he was aware of it. I told him I was still waiting to hear from them, even though it was already a no-go.

"Have you thought about us? Playing here?"

"I did, but I was told there were no scholarships available. And I think I'm ready for change of scenery after being here for four years," I said.

"Yeah, I understand," he said.

Rob Gronkowski was the number-one tight end in the country. I wasn't sure how much playing time I would actually get.

"Well, I'll tell you what," he continued. "You'd be a great redzone target, and we would even double it up sometimes with you and Rob."

It sounded good, but I wasn't convinced, especially after what that assistant of operations had told me previously. But I told Coach Stoops it was something I would like to think about.

"Alright, well, let me know. If you're going to come on board we would need you here by the middle of June to get into our offseason program. Just let me know what you'd like to do."

I still had my mind made up.

"Alright, Coach, will do."

Before he walked off, he said one last thing, "Oh, and there's a scholarship on the table if you want it. So I need to know what's up." He walked towards his office.

Back up... A UA football scholarship?

Just as Coach Stoops dropped the news, Gotch popped up. He was there to meet Stoops at 1:30. My mouth wanted to drop; I couldn't believe he had just offered me a football scholarship on the spot.

I didn't show it, but I was shocked. Very shocked. Stoops was stern and straight to the point. It wasn't a long conversation at all, maybe a few minutes. I was under the assumption the team didn't have any scholarships. But I guess when you talk to the head coach, what he says goes.

I glanced at Gotch with wide eyes. He just smiled at me with an I-told-you-so look, as he followed Stoops into his office.

As I walked back to my car, my mind was racing like crazy. Rice wasn't going to work out, and this offer changed things. I really had to think here.

There was so much uncertainty in my heart.

Why though? I had just been offered a freaking scholarship! Maybe my mind was too caught up with what I had dealt with during hoops. I didn't know why, but something inside me was just holding me back.

I was torn all over again. I couldn't tell anybody about this—namely my dad or Keith. If I didn't accept this offer, I wouldn't have heard the end of it from either one of them. I just needed to pray. Pray and follow my heart to where I believed God was leading it.

The only people who knew about this offer were Gotch, myself, and, of course, Coach Stoops. I knew Gotch wasn't going to push anything on me—he just wanted me to be aware of my options.

The surprise scholarship offer completely changed the game. If I was going to accept the scholarship, I had to drop the showcase and the tryout. Offseason started in June, and those other commitments were in July. It was May.

I had to make a decision fast.

CHAPTER 10

CLARITY

Once the basketball season ended, the entire coaching staff was on the clock. Arizona was searching for a new coach, a successor to Hall of Fame Coach Lute Olson. After a three-week search, the school hired Xavier's head coach, Sean Miller.

I had the pleasure of meeting Coach Miller right before his introductory press conference. He told me he wanted to sit down and meet with me sometime when things settled down. He also told me if I needed help transitioning, he would be more than willing to help. It amazed me because I didn't even know this man, but it showed me what kind of person he was.

Coach Miller brought a couple of coaches with him from his staff at Xavier, which gave me the opportunity to meet James Whitford. Coming into Tucson, Coach Whitford heard about my whole football experience and asked me about it. I filled him in on what had been going on.

I was in the thick of everything, so I didn't even know where to start the story. I told him about the trajectory of my career at UA and how football had come into the picture. Then I told him about the pro day and how nothing came of that.

I explained how I was in limbo between college football and pro ball overseas after the Rice thing didn't work out and how Coach Stoops had just made me an offer. It had been a whirlwind, and I just unloaded everything on him.

After hearing me out, Coach Whitford got quiet. I could tell he was in thought.

Then he looked at me and asked, "Have you ever considered going to the University of Houston to play football?"

"Houston? No, I haven't. It didn't even cross my mind!"

I had looked at Rice because I saw they had just lost their tight end, but I never thought to look at Houston.

He asked if I wanted him to give the Cougar tight ends coach a call on my behalf.

"Sure, if you don't mind," I said.

I wasn't sure if anything would come of it, but it didn't sound like a bad idea.

Coach Whitford hopped on his laptop, began searching for Houston's home football page, and found the tight ends coach.

"Here he is, Tony Levine, tight ends/inside receivers coach. Let me give him a call."

I held my breath, nervously waiting for Levine to pick up. No answer. Coach Whitford left a message on Levine's voicemail and told me he would get back to me as soon as he heard something.

"Thanks, Coach I appreciate it. Let me know if he gets back to you."

A week went by, and I called Coach Whitford to see if he heard anything from Houston. He said he hadn't. It didn't surprise me. I couldn't get anything to go my way when it came to football. Nothing happened from the pro day, I didn't get a camp invite, nor could I get into Rice. I had the scholarship offer, but deep down I didn't want to play at UA. The Seahawks remained silent.

I needed to get away from all this madness.

I decided to go to Fort Collins, Colorado for the Athletes in Action sports ministry camp. I had gone the year before as a camper, and it completely changed my life. This was where I truly became a believer in Christ.

I knew going to camp would be good. I needed to clear my mind and be in a place of peace and solace. JD was the camp director, so I tagged along with him and went as an intern. I needed the time away to just chill and revere the spirit of God. AIA was authentic, real, and the type of environment I needed to be in now.

When word got out that I was coming back, so did word of my football escapades. It was the very thing I was trying to avoid. I didn't want to talk football. I was already stressed, and I wanted to use this time in Colorado to think about something other than football.

I couldn't shake it. Nevertheless, I was able to worship, pour into other athletes as an intern, and use the getaway to clear my mind. Whenever we had free time,

I was in the gym playing pick-up basketball. Surprise, surprise.

It was probably my favorite thing to do behind worship and lunch. This was the first time I had played 5-on-5 basketball since the season ended, and despite the drought, I still had it. I was playing the game I loved, and I did it all week. It reminded me how much I missed it. The more I thought about my situation, the more time I spent in prayer.

I was tired of trying to pursue something I hadn't played since I was a kid. I wasn't even sure if I wanted to play football; I was having so much fun playing basketball.

The football stuff felt forced. It felt like I was running into the same brick wall over and over again. Like I was trying anything I could because of my fear of playing overseas. I couldn't force my way, and I didn't want to any longer.

My time in Fort Collins gave me a better idea of where I was truly leaning. After being there, something inside me made me feel like my decision was already made.

"I think I'm just going to let this football thing go once and for all, JD," I said before I left Colorado.

I was comfortable with that. I let go and let God, and I wanted to see where the round ball would take me.

While I was in Colorado I had been trying to get in touch with Keith. I wanted to get to the bottom of this Seahawks tryout. He got back to me my last day in Fort Collins and texted me the scout's cell phone number. I already had my mind made up, but I decided to contact him anyway, just to see if the tryout had ever been real.

When I called him, he knew exactly who I was. I asked him about the tryout, and he told me they weren't even sure if they were going to do it. It was just something they had talked about.

Wow.

He went on to say that if they did have the tryout, it was unlikely that they would keep any of the participants. It was a quick conversation, but it told me what I needed to know.

This tryout with the Seahawks had seemed fishy from the jump, but it was good to hear it from the horse's mouth. The scout told me that if I wanted to pursue basketball, I would be better off taking those opportunities rather waiting for a "tryout" or a call from them. I agreed, and it gave me that much more confirmation that I was doing the right thing.

That three-minute conversation pretty much concluded my pro football story. There wasn't going to be a Seattle tryout, I couldn't get into Rice, Houston never called back, and I didn't want to play for Arizona. I was on my way back home to Phoenix, and I was going to get ready for this Vegas showcase. I was at peace with everything that happened and the way it happened.

I finally had some closure.

CHAPTER 11

FOR LOVE
OR MONEY

I got back into Tucson, and I was ready to start setting things up for myself in basketball. I had to finishing packing up my apartment, and then I was on my way to Phoenix to start training.

I knew of an overseas agent a friend referred me to, but I didn't want to talk to him while I was pursuing football. Now that I had decided I was sticking with basketball, I was ready to move forward with the process.

I traveled the 115 miles north to Phoenix until I knew what my next move would be.

"Pack your things, Poops," said Dee. "We're leaving."

We're leaving? "Are we going to the beach or back home?" I asked. "Are we going back to Houston?"

"We're leaving here," was all the answer I got.

We had to leave the big white castle hotel and check into another place. We pulled up to the new destination, and the first thing I noticed was the place was much, much smaller. When the taxi dropped us off, I read the sign that stood in front of the building.

MO-TEL.

"What's a motel, Dee?"

I didn't know what it was, but it wasn't anything like the Excalibur. I looked around; there were no lights, no games, and I didn't even see any other people outside. It looked like a raggedy apartment complex.

It wasn't long before we moved to another motel, then another after that. I didn't know what was going on.

My life was dwindling before my eyes. I missed school and my friends. I missed Houston and my dad. We were moving so much, and every place was temporary. I didn't know if we were homeless or running from someone, but, whatever it was, I never felt comfortable or safe.

I always felt like something was wrong, always.

———

I got to Phoenix and started prepping for the basketball showcase. I set up a meeting with Max Berrud, an overseas basketball agent my friend recommended. Max was well-connected and had ties in his home of Paris, as well as Belgium and a few other countries in Europe.

Now that I was at peace with pursuing basketball, I wanted to explore my options. I was working out every day, and it felt really good to get back on the court.

Camp in Colorado had brought out my love for basketball again, and I was ready to focus on that.

I sent my game film to the agent, just as I had sent my football tape to the scouts. He didn't know who I was, but the fact that I was coming out of Arizona helped.

He came to a couple of my training sessions in Scottsdale to meet and evaluate me. After watching my third workout of the week he invited me to play 5-on-5 against some other overseas pros the following week. Things were looking good. Max was like a Godsend.

At the 5-on-5 I held my own against the overseas pros and played really well. Max was ready to sign me right then and there!

"Fenzi, you look good! Real good! I believe you will do very well overseas! Follow me to the car. I have something I want to give you."

He handed me a few sheets of paper. It was a contract to sign with him.

"What's this? A contract?"

"Oui, Monsieur," he replied.

Wow! I told Max I wanted to go home and look over the paperwork myself. I was honored he wanted me to sign with him.

At one point I had been so worried I wouldn't even find a basketball agent, and here I was about to sign with one. The process was *nothing* like the football roller coaster I was just coming off. It reminded me that basketball was what I was meant to do.

When I got home with my contract, I saw that I had missed a call from Coach Whitford. He had left a voicemail.

"Hey Fendi, it's James Whitford. The University of Houston tight ends coach called me back regarding the voicemail we

left a few weeks ago. He left his number and wants you to give him a call…" Whitford left me the coach's name and number.

I hung up the phone.

There was only one word to describe how I was feeling after hearing Coach Whitford's voicemail: disbelief. UH had called back! When we called them and never heard back, I got the clear message that they weren't interested. I had dropped the whole thought of it and moved on.

I figured God had given me *every* sign to show me football was not the route for me. Now this call confused me all over again. I had finally made my mind up that I was going to play pro basketball overseas. I had the contract in my hand!

I didn't even want to flirt with the idea of football again. I had made my mind up.

Right?

I was tired. Tired of being let down by football aspirations and tired of chasing something I had never really done before.

Then it hit me. Maybe that was the problem all along; I was *chasing* it. I thought about all the dead ends I had hit with this football stuff. They were all situations I chased. But this UH one was different.

Nonetheless, I was still over it.

I decided to listen to the voicemail again, and I hesitated for a bit. I was about to delete the message.

Maybe this one would end differently?

No! Leave it alone.

I decided to save the message.

I couldn't figure out if this was another test or an opportunity. I hadn't chased this one. I had put it away once I never heard anything back. God works in mysterious ways! Then this tight ends coach actually called back when I least expected it—just before I was getting ready to sign a basketball contract.

I let a couple of days go by, and I called Coach Whitford back. He told me that Coach Levine, the tight ends coach, sounded very interested. I had heard this before about Rice, so it didn't mean much. But Coach Whitford told me to at least give the coach a call and see what he had to say.

Our compliance guy at Arizona had already given me my release, so I was OK to call Coach Levine. At this point I wasn't sure if I even wanted to call, but I wanted to hear what he had to say.

"Hello, Coach Levine? This is Fendi Onobun. James Whitford told me you left a message a few days ago on his phone."

"Fendi! I was wondering if you were ever going to call! Pleasure to hear from you!"

I could hear the excitement in his voice. He asked me about my situation with basketball and how football came into play. I told him about the roller coaster I was just coming off and mentioned that I was preparing to play basketball professionally overseas.

"Have you signed any contracts yet?" Levine asked.

"I'm actually in the process of signing one with an agent," I responded.

"Can you give me a couple days before you sign that contract?"

Coach Levine asked me to not make any rash decisions. He wanted to make a few calls and see if he could get me in at UH to play football.

"Give me forty-eight hours before you sign that contract and see what I have figured out. Deal?"

"I can do that, Coach. Deal," I replied.

"Great, I'm on it! Talk with you soon."

I really didn't think anything was going to go through, but I had two days to see what this coach was going to come up with. It didn't hurt to wait a couple of days before signing with Max. In the meantime, I continued with my basketball training at Scottsdale Community College.

Max came to the workout and asked me if I had a chance to look over the contract. I told him I was still thinking about it, but really I was just stalling. After the workout, we went out to lunch. He reiterated how I could definitely play professionally overseas.

"Fenzi, you really have the potential to build quickly after your rookie year—you just have to prove yourself. But I've watched you quite a bit, and the ability is there."

It was good to know that I had an agent who was willing to work with me and for me.

Things were looking so good I wasn't sure if the showcase in Vegas would even be necessary anymore. That being said, I still didn't sign any paperwork with Max.

I had given Coach Levine a couple of days, and I didn't want to jump on anything with Max quite yet. Knowing there would be a place for me in a league overseas was reassuring, but I was interested to hear what Levine would come back with.

I told Max that I needed more time; I was exploring some other options. That's when I told him about the football possibility.

"Football!" he responded. "You want to play football? I thought you were a basketball player, Fenzi!"

Through his deep French accent, I could hear how perplexed he was.

"Yeah, I am, Max. But I've been thinking of playing football as well." I told him about the possibility of attending University of Houston to play football and make it to the NFL.

"NFL? Really? Wow! You're some athlete."

Surprisingly, he told me to take my time and let him know what I decided.

"I support you either way you go. You know, I wondered if you played both; you do look like a linebacker… Is that what they call them?"

I laughed. "Yeah, but I'd play tight end."

"I'm more familiar with fútbol… well, people here call it soccer." We both laughed.

Later that evening I called Coach Levine. It had been forty-eight hours since we had spoken, and I wanted to see what he had to say.

When he answered, he got right to business. He told me he had been thinking about my situation and wanted to help me out. He understood I wanted to play basketball. He also understood all the dead ends had turned me away from football. But he asked me to just listen to him.

He had done a little research on me and read about the results of my pro day. He had already seen my YouTube video. Based on that alone, he told me that with some good coaching I could play in the NFL.

"Fendi, you have the size and the ability. Trust me, you can play in the NFL next year. I coached with the Carolina Panthers so I know what it takes. You have it."

He explained that UH had no scholarships left, but he went on, "I will put my all into making sure you become the best tight end you can be. I'll coach you like no other!"

I heard it in Levine's voice: he was dead serious about it. Coming from a man with his NFL coaching experience, that was high praise. I was drawn in by his commitment.

I had only played football once when I was a kid. I hardly understood the game; how was he so sure I'd make it?

"Look, Fendi. We'll get you in over here at Houston. Come home and play for one year, then become a future NFL draft pick in the 2010 draft. *That's* the type of potential you have. You can get picked up with a six-figure signing bonus, next year!"

Compared to being overseas, away from family, making $40,000 to $50,000, it didn't sound like a bad deal. But who was to say I actually would be an *"NFL draft pick with a six figure signing bonus?"* I was a long way from being that.

I had been through the wringer following football opportunities. Those scouts from my pro day, as well as everyone else I had worked with, were saying the same thing Levine was suggesting now.

Why should I trust him?

Coach continued voicing his thoughts and reasons, and I listened hard. I had a lot to think about.

On the one hand, it didn't sound like a bad move. I'd be at home with my family playing for a team on the rise. No one on the Cougar squad had my combination of height, weight, and speed. I'd add a different dimension. When I thoroughly thought about the possibility, it felt like a great opportunity.

On the other, I was skeptical. Yes, it all sounded good, but I had heard it before. I didn't want to pursue another school for it not to work out at the end. And there was no scholarship to make it affordable.

I told Coach Levine I was in the middle of training for a basketball showcase in Las Vegas.

"I hear ya," he said. "Think about what I said. I see potential in you."

"I hear you too, Coach, and it's making a lot of sense to me. I'll think about it, and leave the option open. Can I get back to you in a couple days?"

"Sure, keep me posted," he said.

"Yes, sir," I replied, and we hung up.

I didn't want to tell anyone about UH because I had too many people in my circle as it was. I knew they all meant well, but when their voices overwhelmed me, I wasn't able to make a decision on what *I* wanted to do.

I prayed and asked God again, "What I should do?"

I was clear that if I was going to play football at the college level, I wanted to play in my hometown. Rice hadn't worked out but it looked like Houston would. I had never thought of it as an option, but now it made sense.

I started doing more research on the Cougars. I couldn't believe I was actually doing this. The Vegas showcase was paid for already, because I had been so certain I'd be playing basketball. After talking with Max, I wasn't sure if the showcase was necessary anymore, but since I had already paid the $300, I wanted to go.

As I kept training in Scottsdale, UH was on my mind. I needed to decide quickly if this was something

I wanted to do. Coach Levine had told me from the jump that there were no scholarships available and I didn't have the money to pay for a fifth year of school.

Later that week I missed a call from the Wisconsin area. When I saw it, there was a voicemail for me. A scout from the Green Bay Packers had called, asking me to give him a call ASAP.

Wha-a-a? Is this a prank?

I thought it had to be a prank call. Then I listened again.

The Green Bay Packers? Whoa!

I called him right away.

He had heard about my YouTube video and checked it out. He wanted to come down to Phoenix and put me through a workout.

THIS. WAS. NUTS. Where was all this around the draft?!

I couldn't buy a phone call when I was so interested in getting one, and now that I had decided to stick with hoops, all this was happening. It completely threw me off guard.

"I see some potential in you," said the Packers' scout, "but I want to get a better look."

I was right back in a whirlwind. The scout was Alonzo Highsmith, former NFL player and head college scout for the Green Bay Packers, and he wanted to work me out but Max was getting antsy about contract negotiations, and Coach Levine was trying to persuade me to play a year of football at UH.

"Lord, what do you want me to do?"

Just a week prior, I was 100% sure I was going to play basketball overseas. Now I didn't know what I was going to do.

Trapped in my own uncertainty, I was back at square one.

———————

Dee and I had moved for a fourth time, but this time we were with one of her friends. I was stuck living in some apartment complex with a guy who drove a motorcycle and smoked cigarettes.

Staying there was awful, and I hated it. When I met him, he showed me a bb gun and said, "If you don't behave, there are going to be some problems." That was my introduction to him.

I honestly wanted to give him some problems: that's how much I hated him.

As Dee and I were settling into this new place, I met a few kids playing outside. I tried to stay away from the apartment as much as possible. I wanted out, bad. It had been weeks and I was trapped, trapped in this mess, uncertain if I'd ever see my dad or Houston again.

All I wanted to do was go back home.

"Dee, when are we going back home?!" I begged. "I hate it here!"

No response.

A couple weeks went by, and I realized these neighborhood kids weren't the goody two-shoes type. They were much older than me, but I was just as big as them, so no one ever asked my age.

We did all kinds of mischievous things around the complex, things I had never dreamed of doing. The day before Christmas, we filled up a bunch of glass ornaments with egg yolks and threw them at doors. Another day we TP'd the complex trees with toilet tissue.

I told the kids about the bb gun the guy had in the apartment. We went to look for it, but we couldn't find it.

A couple of days later, the gun went missing. The motorcycle dude went berserk. I didn't know how it had disappeared, but I didn't care. He kicked Dee and me out of his place shortly after that and we were on the move again, looking for another place to stay.

———————

I called Coach Levine and told him the news about the scout from the Packers. That only ignited his efforts to get me into the UH program.

I felt like I was dreaming. None of this felt real. Mr. Highsmith wanted to set up a day to put me through a workout in Phoenix. After our initial conversation, he wanted to know how I had even gotten into football in the first place, and what brought me to this point. It took a few conversations to unravel the whole story, but he began to understand why I had made the decisions that led me here.

"At the end of it, sir," I explained to him, "I think the thing that hurt me the most was my inexperience. So I decided to continue with the basketball training."

Mr. Highsmith and I kept in touch and spoke on the phone almost daily. We'd go back and forth on things, then after we had gone a little deeper during one of our conversations, he said, "Look, Fendi, I could fly out and put you through a workout and bring you into Green Bay. You would have an opportunity to make our practice squad, but I wouldn't want you to risk that. The NFL can be cutthroat, and you don't have much experience. I'm thinking for the long term."

"If you want to pursue football, your best route would be to go to school for a year and play. Get some film, learn the game, and gain some experience." Then he added, "You would definitely raise your chances of making it to the pros."

I understood what he was saying, but I reminded him I didn't have a good school option. I didn't want to go to UA, Rice was out, and UH didn't have any scholarships.

I hadn't told him about Houston but he said, "If you could go to school and get at least twenty catches and block well, you'd get invited to the combine. That's huge! It's just a better route for you to go, Fendi. Trust me."

If pro football was something I really wanted to do, I knew Highsmith was right. From what I had quickly learned, it was the only path that made sense. He was trying to help me think about the longevity of a "possible" football career.

I just had to figure out if pro football was something I wanted to do.

For real this time.

I continued to work out my body on the hardwood every day in Scottsdale, while my mind was busy thinking about UH. Max wanted to get things rolling with the contract, and the time to make some big decisions was looming.

I picked up the phone and called David Griffin at the Phoenix Suns. When I did my internship with them, he and I had developed a good relationship. I asked him if they had any roster spots on their summer league team.

The NBA draft had already passed, and their summer league was right around the corner. Most teams fill their summer league rosters with rookie draft picks and young players or guys who need more development.

Sometimes there is a spot or two for a guy who may not play much but could be an add-on to the roster. These players will more than likely end up playing in the Developmental League or overseas, but the exposure helps them improve. I thought I could get a crack at one of those spots.

As if I didn't have enough going on. But I figured the least I could do was ask.

When I called Griff, he said they didn't have a spot on their summer league roster. But he had heard about me pursuing football. He asked how that was going, it felt like the hundredth time I had to tell my story.

I started at the beginning and told him about all the setbacks I experienced and where I was at the moment trying to pursue a basketball career overseas. I told him the whole story, and I found myself telling him about the University of Houston opportunity.

He was the first person I had talked about it with, and I explained my uncertainty, since they didn't have any scholarships available.

Once he heard that, he stopped me right there. The tone of the conversation shifted. I could hear the seriousness in his voice as he began talking about opportunities, taking risks, and never having any "what ifs" in life.

Griff brought up something important in our conversation. "Fendi, in life you have to make business decisions. When opportunities such as this one at UH come about, you have to take advantage of them. You could definitely make a living playing basketball—but do you just want to be making a living in some other country?" He paused before continuing, "Or do you want to have a chance to be the next prototypical tight end in the NFL for years to come? Fendi, you have that kind of ability."

Everything looked different when he explained it as a business decision. I realized that I had been playing not to lose; I hadn't been playing to win.

"Try football out for a year," said Griff. "Basketball overseas isn't going anywhere. If it doesn't work out, you have a plan B. But doing something as lucrative as playing pro football should be worth more risk than just making a living."

Griff made sense. I had a bridge (UH) that provided a wonderful opportunity to potentially play football at the highest level in the world (NFL). Why wouldn't I cross it to discover what lay on the other side? If it didn't work out, I had a solid plan B.

"You are an uncommon breed, and most guys with your ability are in the NFL. Fendi, I'm telling you, at the very least try it out. See how you like it. You will never know unless you try."

Although I had come to understand how limited my understanding of football was, I knew there were a lot of athletic basketball players who had made the transition. Going to school for a year to create a better opportunity to succeed at the next level was a make-or-break chance. Scholarship or not. Griff had a point.

"You don't want to look back when you're thirty-five years old and say, 'What if I had played football when I had the chance? Where would I be today? Look at this opportunity as an investment; since it's unlikely they will give you a scholarship, invest into yourself. Take out a school loan. That's what I mean by making this a business decision. The only outcome for you in all this should be making it to the NFL."

I thanked Griff for his perspective. When I hung up, I put some serious thought into our conversation. Yes, I wanted to play basketball, but being able to try football as a chance of a lifetime seemed too good to pass up.

There weren't too many people who had the opportunity to walk onto a football team after playing basketball their entire lives and give themselves the chance to make it to the NFL.

I called Coach Levine, and he reinforced that he would make it his job for me to become an NFL tight end. He added that it would be his personal duty to speed up my learning curve and work with me daily to ensure I left UH more prepared than ever for the next level.

I was now seriously considering this route. I didn't like the idea of loans, but this was going to be a business decision.

Coach Levine had said, "If everything works according to plan, the loan you would need to take out for a fifth year here at Houston could all be paid off with a small piece of your signing bonus after you sign your first contract in 2010."

It all sounded good. If I was going to make this move, it was because I believed in my ability to make it to the NFL. God opened a door for me that I never forced.

I made a pros and cons list of going home to play football for UH versus going overseas for basketball. I looked at every angle, and it was a long process.

When I finished, there were more pros for football.

One big consideration was that I had money lined up overseas in basketball, and hoping to make money in the NFL was more of a risk. But now the thought of going for it was very intriguing to me.

The conversation with Griff was a turning point. He showed me that I had a chance of a lifetime. In order to be successful and reach that goal, I'd have to take that risk. And I'd have to believe in my ability to handle that risk.

I made a business decision, insured by my belief in my God-given abilities. If it didn't work out, I would have basketball in my back pocket. I was going walk on and play football at the University of Houston.

I was going home.

Now I had to let Max know my decision. I told him I wanted to meet with him to let him know what was going on. It felt strange because the reason I had contacted Max in the first place was because I had been so sure I was done with the football chase.

"Fen-zee, do whatever you feel is best for you. If it doesn't work out, I would love the opportunity to work for you and find basketball opportunities overseas."

Relief rushed in. After the rollercoaster ride of the last few months, I had made my decision, and I had a clear direction plus a basketball agent in my back pocket if I needed it.

CHAPTER **12**

H-TOWN BOUND

I felt fully committed to the idea of playing football at UH. It just felt right. The Cougars were coming off a decent year finishing 8-5 under first-year Head Coach Kevin Sumlin and were favored to win their division the in the upcoming season. They also had an awesome quarterback, Case Keenum, who was second in the nation in total passing yards. He was the face of the program and their best player.

Houston was definitely a pass-happy offense, and they had just lost their leading receiver, who was a tight end. Yes, a tight end! So the spot was open for the taking!

I still hadn't talked to anyone about this besides Griff. My dad was under the assumption that I was pursuing pro basketball overseas, as was everyone else. Under NCAA regulations, Coach Levine was only allowed one phone call to me. If I wanted to talk to him, I had to contact him.

"Hello, Coach Levine, it's Fendi Onobun. I've got some news for you... I want to come to Houston. I want to play football for you guys."

"You serious?" he asked.

"Yes sir!" I assured him. "I'm ready."

"Fendi, you won't regret it. I promise ya. We're excited to have you! I'll get you connected with our academic advisor tomorrow."

Coach Levine was stoked, and so was I. This was a risk, but I wanted to see if I could actually play this game. I knew I had a ways to go, but I wanted it and I was committed. What better way to make a dream come true? For me, this was it.

I was ready to take my business trip down to Houston.

I decided to forego the Vegas showcase. My mind was made up, and I canceled my plans to go. The only thing I was focused on now was UH football.

Coach Levine used his one call to connect me with the team's academic adviser, Maria Peden, known as MC. She told me I qualified for enrollment, but I needed to get accepted into a graduate program.

Since I was a transfer student, the same rules applied as when I tried to get into Rice. I had to get into a program at UH that was not offered at UA. In three short weeks, I completed the application process for graduate school, applied for financial aid, wrote my letter to the NCAA for my transfer, and took the grad school entrance exam.

Only after I had completed all of that was when I told my dad what I had decided to do.

"Dad, I'm going to play football at the University of Houston. I'm going to use my fifth year of eligibility and play. I'm already in talks with them and I've completed the application process."

"Wow!" he said. "Really?"

"Yes, sir!" I answered happily.

"I'm proud of you," he said. "I think that's a very good decision."

And when I told him "I'm coming back home!" he admitted, "I was nervous about you going overseas to play basketball."

The best thing about this decision was the peace I had in my heart about it. After all the talks and conversations, it felt like a God-driven situation. Now all I had to do was wait on clearance into the graduate program. I had done everything on my part, and I was pretty confident I would get in.

Coach Levine wanted me to come down to Houston and meet Coach Sumlin. He also wanted me to meet the other offensive coaches, a few players, and watch the team play 7-on-7. I gladly accepted.

My dad bought me a plane ticket to Houston so we could meet Coach Levine for the first time. When we got together at the alumni center on campus, Coach Levine said, "Well you must be our new tight end! Pleasure to meet you, Fendi!"

"Nice to finally meet you, too, Coach!" I replied sincerely.

I couldn't believe I was at UH taking an unofficial football visit, like this was actually happening! Levine didn't waste any time, and we got right to business. I had a plethora of people to meet and not a lot of time, so we were moving fast.

Coach Levine gave my father and me a tour of their facility. I got a chance to see all the football film rooms, meeting rooms, and their weight room. When we entered the weight room, I heard a deep voice say, "Now this guy looks like a football player!" It was Coach Larry Jackson, Houston's head strength and conditioning coach.

"Coach Jackson, this is Fendi Onobun and his father James. He's taking an unofficial visit with us at the moment. Basketball player from Arizona."

As Levine introduced me, Jackson's eyes lit up. "Oh, wow! Okay! He's coming here, Levine?"

"We're workin' on it. Hoping he can be our tight end next year."

Jackson smiled. "Pleasure to met you, Fendi and Mr. Onobun. Fendi, hopefully we can get you here and in our program!"

I watched the guys on the team work out for a bit, but no one in there had my stature. I still couldn't believe I was touring to play football; it seemed so surreal to me.

After meeting Coach Jackson, my father and I had lunch, then came back to meet with Head Coach Kevin Sumlin. He was happy to hear that I wanted to be a part of the program.

"We have something special brewing here at Houston. We can help you, and you can help us. I know what the plan is, and Levine has already told me he's going to get you ready to play come fall. To me it's a win-win situation."

My father and I felt the same way.

Coach Sumlin said he knew of me from my Alief Taylor days when he recruited my friend and high school basketball teammate Martellus Bennett in 2005. Sumlin was the tight ends coach at Oklahoma at the time

"I remember when you were just a pup in high school," he said. "I saw your athleticism and was wondering why you weren't playing football then. You have a lot of potential and you could come in here and really help us. You'll have a chance to play at the next level; we'd just have polish you up first. You can be that good, despite your learning curve."

That was high praise coming from him. Everyone saw the potential, and that was the reason I was there: to turn potential into reality.

The meeting with Coach Sumlin gave me a better idea of how he saw me and what I could do for the team. Once we finished, Coach Levine and I went into the film room. My dad left for a couple of hours while I watched film with Levine. He wanted to teach me their offense and break down some film.

"Do you know what the line of scrimmage is and how many players are on it?"

I looked at him with a blank stare. "No sir, I don't."

"It's OK, this will be like teaching my two-year-old son the game of football," he said with a chuckle. He knew I had a long way to go, but he also seemed like he knew I was going to be fine.

I was nervous.

Coach Levine started with the basics from the offensive side of the ball. Luckily, in their offense, the tight end position was easy to learn and play.

"For the offense there are eleven players on the field, seven of which are on the line of scrimmage— the imaginary line that is made once the ball has been downed from the previous play." He walked me through step by step.

"The ball always starts with the center, who is always in the middle of the line. To the right and left of the center are the right and left guard, then to the right of the guard is the right tackle and to the left of the guard is the left tackle. We now have five players on the line. The quarterback is behind the center, sometimes closer or further, but he's not a player on the line.

"Then there is usually a running back, or an 'H' back, and that makes him the seventh player on offense. After that there are three receivers." The he turned to me and asked, "How many players are on the field?"

"Ten, Coach."

"That's correct."

I was looking at the whiteboard, trying to follow along as Coach Levine drew each position. "The eleventh and final player is here on the end, next to the tackle, and this will be you, the tight end. That makes eleven players."

"Oh, OK. I got it," I told him. "So is it always set up like this?"

"No, the formation will determine the number of backs, receivers or tight ends on the field, and if they are on or off the line, because they are all subject to change. The usual five offensive linemen are never off the line. There are only changes in the receivers and backs."

"Got it," I said.

"I don't want to confuse you, but I wanted to show you the basic set up; you'll learn all the other stuff later."

I had about a thousand questions. This was all new to me. Growing up, I was such a basketball nut that I rarely watched football: I knew everything about basketball and literally nothing about football. I felt like I had the IQ of a five-year-old while Levine was talking, but I continued to take notes and follow along.

After the tutorial we watched film on a few basic offensive concepts. I also watched a lot of their tight drills and plays from spring ball.

"You're going to play 'Y,'" he said. "That's the tight end in our offense." Levine and I watched all the clips of the Y from the spring game, and we watched the blocking drills as well. I couldn't wait to see myself on film making those same catches in just a few months.

"Alright Fendi, I don't want to overload you on your visit. I think you have a good foundation of our concepts and the tight end position. We'll build from here."

I definitely knew a lot more going out of that room than I did going in.

We walked outside to the practice field where the team was getting ready to play 7-on-7. Coach introduced me to a few guys on the team since regulations wouldn't allow him to stay out there. One the guys I met was Wesley Scourten, another tight end on the team. Wes was battling a foot injury but was out there watching the 7-on-7.

Levine told me to hang with Wes while he went back inside.

"Welcome back to the H, man," said Wes.

"I appreciate it," I replied.

"I heard you just started playing football."

"Yeah, man, I'm trying to pick it up."

"I got you. I'll show you what the guys are working on now." Wes started explaining all the different hand signals and plays. I was able to follow a little bit, but there was so much going on. And this was 7-on-7! They were moving fast—it wasn't like I was watching pick-up basketball. This was whole new animal.

Afterwards I got a chance to meet a few more of the players briefly before I went back inside to conclude my visit.

"Fendi, it's been a pleasure to have you here," Coach Levine said. "I'm glad you were able to come out and see us, and we're looking forward to you being here." He looked to my dad. "Mr. Onobun, thank you again. We are really excited about your son."

"Oh, Coach, we thank you for giving him the opportunity," my dad replied. "We are extremely grateful."

"Coach, thanks for the football 101," I said. "I can't wait to get started!"

My trip to Houston was a good one. I felt like I was making the right move, and I was confident Coach Levine would bring me up to speed. The plan he had made me feel that I would end up being just fine with him as my coach. My father thought UH was a good fit as well, especially after talking with Coach Sumlin.

After my recruiting experience in high school, my dad and I were well aware of the process. We also knew how coaches swooned athletes, but being twenty-two, I was a lot smarter this go-round. I believed Houston had some plans for me.

I didn't know much about football, so I truly didn't understand all the intricacies of their offense. But their tight end had been their leading receiver the previous year, and that was good enough for me. They understood what I was trying to do and what the end goal was.

For me this was a business trip. I wanted to learn the game and prepare myself for the next level. I was committed to the transition and wanted to give my all to this.

While I was there, Levine told me he thought it would be best for me get back to Houston as soon as possible. He wanted me to spend time at the facility watching film, learning the game, and playing 7-on-7 with the team.

The only problem was that I hadn't heard from the school about my acceptance yet. I was skeptical about moving without any notice, so I wasn't sure about making the 1100-mile drive from Phoenix. It was a risk.

Then I thought back to what Griff told me about taking risks. I didn't want to just sit and wait. I had a lot to learn in a little bit of time

When I got back to Arizona, I began planning my move back to Houston. I couldn't believe I was going ahead with this, but I knew what I wanted to do—finally. This was an investment, and I was 100 percent sure I was going to do it.

Coach Levine plugged me in with Lorenzo Diamond, one of his former players who was now a football coach at Scottsdale Community College—the same place I had been training for basketball just the week before. He had played tight end for Levine when he was a coach at Auburn, then played in the NFL for a couple seasons.

I got a chance to work with Coach Diamond for a few days before I left for Houston. There was so much to learn about being a tight end, let alone about the game itself! My brief time with him really opened my eyes.

It had been a while since I had spoken with Keith, and I wanted to update him on the news. I gave him a call. "So guess what, man?

"What's up?" he asked, glad to hear from me.

"I'm going to University of Houston to play football for my fifth year of eligibility!"

"Wh-a-a-a-t? Since when?" I could tell how surprised he was.

"Well, I've been working on it for the past month or so now. I leave in a few days and wanted to let you know."

"Wow, man! That's exciting! Are you serious? That's great, Fendi!"

"Well," I told him, "You guys started all this football talk. We'll see where it goes."

"Ha ha, we will! But I honestly thought you were done with it," he said. "Billy will be happy to hear about this."

I left for Houston on July 15th. There a few things still unknown, but I had faith I was moving in the right direction, that I had made the right decision.

I was actually moving back home to play collegiate football! No more basketball.

I left my basketball and basketball shoes in storage, and once the car was packed I was off to Houston. It was good to see my family. Once I got settled at my parents' house I went to UH to get myself acclimated.

I spent three hours a day watching film in the meeting room and learning all of the team's plays. I was starting from the ground up. I had been away from Houston for almost five years, so it also felt like I was in a foreign town.

I knew God had brought me here, and I wanted to rely on Him to carry me through this new experience.

When the motorcycle guy kicked us out, Dee and I started looking for another place to stay. I was happy about leaving; I hated that guy so much.

Dee and I made our way back to the motel we were staying at before we moved in with the crazy guy. We had only been away for a few weeks, but the motel felt more like home than anything else at this point.

"We're back," Dee said when we walked up to the door.

I had the bag full of toys I had been dragging all around Las Vegas. She opened the door, and I walked into the weird-smelling room.

Was I ever going to see my dad again?

"Does my dad know we're here?" I asked her suspiciously.

"Yes," she said.

Something didn't feel right, but there wasn't much I could do.

A box motel room in Las Vegas was my new life; this was my home; welcome back.

The following week I started a workout regimen at my new school. By NCAA regulations, I was not allowed to work out with the team, because I wasn't officially a student there yet. So I did workouts on my own.

It was tough, but I found a way to get it done. I developed a routine for myself after my first week. During voluntary 7-on-7, I'd watch to pick up on the plays. I didn't have the whole offense down, but I had enough to play.

The offense drove the ball to the 5-yard line. "Fendi, come on out here!" Case called me to come in at the Y. I was thrown right into the fire.

I saw the hand signal and lined up in the slot. I had a fade route to the back pylon. The defense's top cornerback was there to cover. I think everyone out there knew the ball was coming my way. The squad wanted to see what I was made of.

"Go-o-o-o, Hit!"

I took off and bolted towards the back right pylon. As I made my cut, the DB broke towards the direction I was going. I looked up and saw the ball. I jumped as high as I could and tried to grab it like a rebound. I had it in my hands but on the way down it was ripped right out.

Incomplete pass. The cornerback got up.

"LET'S GO, D!! WASSUP!"

That was my first shot, and I had wanted to do something with it. Unfortunately, it didn't happen.

Dang!

Case came up to me. "It's OK, big guy. We'll get plenty more of those."

By my second week I had a better grasp on the offense. It was a lot coming at me, but the guys on the team were helping me out. I spent a lot of time with Tyron Carrier and James Cleveland. They showed me the ropes and took me under their wing.

They were different, and you saw it by how hard they worked. Their play stood out from everyone else's on the field, and they were selfless guys. My learning curve was obvious, and both Tyron and James told me whatever I needed, they'd help. No questions asked.

It was as if they already knew why I was there, and where I was trying to go.

For the rest of July, those two didn't waste any time. Every day after 7-on-7 they would spend nearly three hours honing my skills. We worked on technique, route running, hand placement, body positioning, and catching—you name it, we worked on it.

Working with those two became part of my regimen, and we did it all summer. They were special. Tyron was coming off of a great sophomore season as the second leading receiver on the team and first-team All-Conference selection. James was a junior college transfer who was a JUCO All-Conference player.

The extra work I was putting in was beginning to pay off. I still had my difficulties, but I kept working. I was thinking about everything I had to do on the field, every move I made, but this was truly a transition.

The more 7-on-7 I played, the more comfortable I got. I still couldn't believe I was playing football, and I was actually having fun with it. This was nothing but God.

By the end of July, I was already seeing results. I saw it in my route running and the way I was reading the backers off the line. The knowledge I gained from James and Tyron was showing.

On the last day of voluntary 7-on-7, the second string QB threw me the same fade route Case had thrown me on my first day. It was the same exact set up.

This time around, I was able to sell a different route and make the corner bite with a head nod at the top of my route. I ran it more precisely this time as I angled myself towards the back right pylon.

I looked up and saw the ball floating in the air. Once I was in the air, I reached up with my left hand and snagged the football one-handed over the cornerback's head. When it hit my hands, I held onto it for dear life, clenching it to my chest on my way down.

TOUCHDOWN!

The team went crazy! Game over. I shut it down.

"OK! Now this is what we need on our team!" They were all buzzing.

"Good catch, Fifty!" one of the receivers said. I looked at him, wondering what he meant by "Fifty." "Yes, Fifty, not Fendi, because you got a fifty-inch vertical!"

All the guys surrounded me with cheers and high fives.

"Break us down, Fifty!" The team began walking toward the huddle, fists clenched, ready for me to break it.

"Alright!" I shouted. "Hard work on three! One, two, three, HARD WORK!"

I knew, before I made the move to Houston, if I wanted to amount to anything on this team, I was going to have to work hard. All the hard work I had put in was what allowed me to make that play.

We had a week off before we started camp, so I had to make sure I was ready. I didn't want to take time off, so I continued to work during that week. James and Tyron were working with me, too, and giving me the rundown about camp.

"Fen, two-a-days is all about football—morning, noon, and night," they explained. "You're going to be eating, sleeping, and dreaming about football. Make sure you're mentally and physically ready. It's a grind."

During the off week, I was at home getting ready for workouts, when I received an e-mail from the School of Technology. I knew right away what it was—my admittance email.

I opened it from my iPhone and downloaded the attached letter. I was so excited. I skimmed across the top of the letter:

Dear Mr. Onobun,

The University of Houston School of Technology is sorry to inform you that we cannot accept you into our ...

My heart dropped to my stomach.
What?!
I read it again slowly to make sure I clearly saw the words again. *Sorry* and *cannot.* I couldn't believe what I was reading. I was furious.

I had moved my things from Arizona. I was asked and advised to come to Houston early, trusting that I would get into the school. I had been working my tail off on the field.
And now this?
I didn't know what to do.

The first person I called was MC, the team's academic advisor. As soon as I told her the bad news, she was already getting on her other phone to make calls. MC told me she would call me right back.
Did I make the right decision doing this?
As fast as she started making calls, I started second-guessing my decision to come to Houston. I started making plans for how I was going to get back to Arizona to see Max.

I felt so stupid. I even started questioning God.

Why would You bring me down here for this?

There was so much going through my mind, I couldn't even think straight. More than anything, I was disappointed.

I called Coach Levine and told him news. He was already aware of it, but he didn't seem as panicked as I felt. "Hey, we got everybody in academics working on it. Stay put in Houston," he counseled me. "We'll get it squared away."

I was upset, but I stayed put.

Levine told me to keep up with my routine until further notice. I had a hard time staying motivated with the unknown. Then Coach Sumlin called me and told me he was getting right on it.

That was a little more comforting, but I was still worried and had a million questions. I felt like all the work I had put in was for nothing.

I turned to my Bible, looking for answers.

Matthew 6:32-34 NLT says, 32: These things dominate the thoughts of unbelievers but your heavenly Father already knows all your needs. 33: Seek first the Kingdom of God above all else and live righteously and he will give you everything you need. 34: So don't worry about tomorrow, for tomorrow will bring its own worries. Today's trouble is enough for today.

As upset and concerned as I was, when I turned to my faith, I was reminded that God had opened this door. I was going to continue to walk through it confidently. Whatever was going to happen with the situation was going to happen.

I knew if I kept my faith, God would provide. While remaining faithful, it was hard for me to sleep that night. In the morning, I wasn't very motivated to drive to UH and do my workout, but I made myself get out there. I needed to get my mind off of the situation.

I knew training with James and Tyron would take my mind off of the situation. Working with them so much, a real friendship had developed. They both had a crazy work ethic, and we really respected each other. Getting out there with them that day was the best thing I could have done.

When I got home after the workout, I saw I had a missed call and a voicemail from MC. I listened to it ASAP.

"Hi Fendi, it's MC. We have good news! The grad school reversed its decision and you have been accepted under conditional circumstances of maintaining a 3.0 GPA, which I know won't be difficult for you. Congratulations! You're a Houston Cougar!

I was so relieved when I got the news. I was officially a student at UH and a member of the football team. All I could do was thank God.

Now my focus was getting ready for two-a-days.

CHAPTER 13

TWO-A-DAYS

In my locker, there was a red practice jersey with the number "*81*" on it. When I saw that number hanging in my locker, it felt divine and purposeful, like this was all meant to be.

This was definitely going to be a different look for me; I never had a number so high in my life!

The fact that 81 was available gave me more of a reason to believe this was God's plan. In the Bible the number eight means new beginnings. And one for me symbolized my most important audience—God. This was a new beginning for sure, and my faith had carried me through to this point.

We had our first official team meeting that day. I was amazed at how many guys were sitting in the meeting room. There had to be close to a hundred guys in there.

After the meeting with Coach Sumlin, we broke up into unit meetings. Offense met in one room, and defense met in the other. From there, we had position meetings. We had seven inside receivers and five tight ends.

I was happy to see my boys James and Tyron in the room; they were both inside receivers. Coach Levine walked in the room, whipped out six bags of sunflower seeds, and threw them in the middle of the table for grabs. I sat between Wes and James.

Levine passed out the script for the first day of practice.

"If you need any help with the plays, I got ya, Big Dog," Wes told me.

I looked at the script and started reading through plays. A lot of them looked familiar, but there was a lot on there I'd never seen before.

Levine went over the script in detail. "Fendi," he pointed out to me, "any play with a 12 next to it means you're in. That's 12 personnel, which means two-tight ends."

I knew the plays; now I had to put the pieces into action on the field—that was going to be the interesting part. After the meetings, the offensive coordinator, Dana Holgorsen, pulled me to the side.

"We're going to take things slow and progress you bit by bit, 81."

He expressed that he knew why I was here, but, with me being so new to the game, he didn't want to overwhelm me with all their plays. "As a tight end, there are only a few things NFL scouts need to see you do. They want to see you run block, run a couple routes, and show your ability to catch the football."

Dana told me I would have the opportunity to eventually do that, but for now I needed to focus on the few plays that were run out of 12 personnel, which weren't many.

I came to UH to play, that was why I had worked so hard learning the offense with Levine. But I understood where he was coming from. This was going to be my *first* time playing football at this level. I didn't have a lot of time and I still had a lot to learn. Hopefully I could progress fast.

After the meetings, I went down to the equipment room and picked up my gear. They gave me my helmet, shoulder pads, cleats, and practice pants—the whole bit.

As the equipment guy checked the fit for my shoulder pads, I caught a glimpse of myself in a mirror. I almost didn't recognize my reflection; I looked huge with the pads on.

I *still* couldn't believe I was doing this. I just laughed. I was so used to seeing myself in basketball uniforms, it felt like I was looking at a stranger.

I'm football player now… I couldn't stop laughing when I thought about it—unbelievable.

I took all the equipment to my locker. This truly felt like God. I was so thankful. Things were coming into fruition.

That night we had a team dinner, and, after dinner, it was off to the house. I had to get rested for my first official two-a-day the next morning.

I woke up bright and early, ready to go. I was definitely excited. Breakfast was at 7:30 a.m., and then we had meetings at 9.

Surprisingly, I didn't have first day jitters. I went to the locker room to look at the schedule and noticed we had to take team pictures and speak to media. I *thought* we had practice.

My mind was ready to get on field today, but it was just media day.

Shaking my head...

I walked towards my locker and there hung the scarlet and white game jersey! It read "HOUSTON" across the front in white capital letters and had a big "81" right in the middle of the jersey below. The back read "Onobun," stitched in white capital letters, with a bigger 81 to go with it.

U of H Football Media Day. August 2009.

It was a thing of beauty.

I was so excited to put it on. A milestone in my brand-new football career. I took my iPhone out and started snapping pictures out of pure excitement, but quickly snapped back into reality, remembering I had team pictures to take.

When I was fully dressed in my new uniform, I took one last peek at myself in the mirror.

I'm a football player now.

Now all I had to do was learn how to actually play the game!

August 7, 2009, was our first actual two-a-day practice. Breakfast was at 7:30 and I was taped and ready to go by 8:45. I hadn't seen or been in a football practice since I was thirteen, and I didn't know what to expect.

I was about to find out quickly—this was on-the-job training.

When 9 a.m. arrived, I was on the practice field. We finished warm-ups by 9:10. Coach Sumlin blew his whistle, and then all the players scattered to their stations.

I didn't know where to go.

"Somebody point Fendi to where he's supposed to be!" Coach Sumlin yelled. "He's lost!"

"Over here, 81!" Levine yelled.

We started off in a station with the offensive line to work on blocking drills and techniques. There were guys in front of us with dummy blocking bags to act as a defense. I was working with the second string. I got in my stance and waited for the first sound.

"Hit!"

I lunged out towards the dummy bag and pushed it out to simulate my block.

"Whoa, Fendi, your steps! Your steps! They're too long! You won't have any power, stepping like that," Levine said "Take six-inch steps, and make contact on your second step. Punch the bag; don't lunge at it."

It was evident this was my first time blocking. It felt so weird pushing this bag. This was definitely going to be a learning process. It wasn't going to be easy, either. I knew if this was going to work, it was going to take repetitions, patience, and *a lot* of practice.

This was only day one, rep one—I had time to get better.

"If you need help with anything, I got you," Justin told me. Justin Johnson, aka Juice, was our H-back flex tight end. He was the utility guy who did it all, and was extremely knowledgeable about the game.

With him doing everything before me, I was able to watch all of his reps. I could tell he knew what he was doing. Anytime I had a problem with something, Juice had no problem helping me out.

Levine coached me up each and every day, and kept his word on helping me become the best tight end I could possibly be.

"Your blocking is getting better every day," he said. "Keep working at it."

The more reps I got in practice, the better. Run blocking wasn't feeling as uncomfortable anymore. As days went by, my confidence began to rise. I was spending time in Levine's office watching film, and he continued to give me tips and coaching points. I made small notes to myself and made sure I took whatever we talked about to the field.

Watching myself on film and seeing the improvement everyday was motivating. I was taking the first steps in becoming a football player—one building block at a time.

In practice I really didn't get to see the ball much, but I knew in time that would come. The other tight ends and I worked on routes with Levine, but the majority of our work consisted of blocking.

I was one week into camp and my body was *sore*!

Another adjustment for me was the lifting program; we lifted a lot heavier, for sure. During my time at Arizona, we rarely lifted heavy weights. Being on a football team, we *had* to lift, and we did Olympic-style lifting, which was new to me as well.

I was lifting more weight than I ever had before. I was sore in muscles I didn't even know existed, but I could already feel the growth in my body from the explosive style of lifting.

Tyron was right—two-a-days were a grind. With all the meetings, running, and lifting before and after practice, my first week in camp had me dead. I had never been through anything like this before.

I improved a lot during the first week of camp in addition to watching film with Coach Levine. He continued teach me the ins and outs of the position during meetings, and then I would watch more film with the tight ends as a group.

Almost instantly from the first practice to the sixth, I could see my improvement.

My technique was better, and I was taking quicker steps on the block. I actually looked like I knew what I was doing on film. I wanted to be the best tight end in our group by the end of camp. That was my goal.

I was having a blast learning my new craft. My body was hurting, but I knew I was getting better each day, and that's what kept me going.

By practice seven, we were finally fully padded. It was crazy how big I looked on the field compared to my teammates. I felt like a giant.

"You're huge, 81!"

I thought I would be super heavy with all the equipment on, but I hardly felt any different. We had been practicing in shoulder pads for the last couple of days, so adding the pants didn't make much of a difference. One thing I did know was that full pads meant full go: practice was going to be more physical today, and I was going to have to come with it in the blocking drills.

We were eight practices in, and I couldn't tell you *exactly* what I was doing when it came to blocking. But whatever it was, it was working. I got better with each rep and I was winning my rep every time.

"Goo-o-od, Fendi! Stay low! Drive! Drive!" I was applying the notes from the film room to the field, and everything Levine was telling me to do was working.

Toward the end of practice, we had a fifteen-play scrimmage, full contact. It would be my first time in a game-type setting. I had two plays in the scrimmage.

My first play was a zone run to the left, with me on the backside block. My job was to cut off the defensive end from making the play.

Easy money. Every time I was on the backside of this play, it felt like I was driving hard left for a dunk. I would take a step with my left foot, lean and stay low, just like I was blowing by a defender. The difference was I could shoot my hands up to stop the defender and make the block.

I was killing our left defensive end in practice. One of the scout team guys told me the D-line coach was always in his grill because he couldn't get around my blocks. I had only been playing football for a week!

I was still being called the "basketball guy" by some of the defensive coaches, but I was holding my own, and I loved it.

A few plays later my formation was called again.

"Deuce! Deuce!"

I ran onto the field and saw the quarterback's hand signal. I had a drag route. I finally had a chance to get the ball! The play was 95 drag. I knew exactly what I was supposed to do.

I got in my three-point stance on the line waiting for the quarterbacks' cadence.

"Go, Hit!"

I got off the line, climbed up eight yards, passing the Sam linebacker. Then, I ran up five more behind the Mike linebacker. I crossed the field at fifteen yards, running as fast as I could, looking for Case to throw me the ball.

The ball ended up going to the other tight end who had the flat route to the sideline. He caught it and took off running. I was sprinting towards him as I saw the weak side linebacker chasing to make a tackle.

I caught up to the backer and shoulder blocked him as hard as I could to knock him out of the way before he could tackle Tyler.

A whistle blew.

"Fendi! What in the hell are you doing?!" Coach Sumlin yelled.

"That's a 15-yard penalty for clipping. You can't do that! Block from the back!"

Dumbfounded, I thought I was making a play, when actually, I had done something that took away the yards we had just gained. I had no idea. Clearly, I had a lot to learn about the rules of the game.

Embarrassing.

When I clipped the backer I heard some guys from the defense laughing. "Big basketball player don't know what he's doing out there."

I really had no idea.

When I jogged back to the sideline, our offensive co-ordinator was smiling at me, cracking up. "It's all right. You'll be fine, good effort. But for future reference, you can't block, push, or clip a defensive player in the back when they are ahead of you. You have to be able to see their front jersey number before you make a block like that on the run."

"Yes sir," I responded.

As humiliating as that penalty was, I went and bought *Football for Dummies* that same day and vowed to never make that mistake again.

My mistake also led me to more film study, and it didn't take long before I was watching NFL games religiously on Sundays. Any time I saw a tight end on TV, I glued my eyes to him the entire game. I was trying to study the things they did and emulate their techniques on the field. I planned on being there one day.

We were at practice number eleven of two-a-days, and I had a good routine by now. My days were mostly football. We met, lifted, napped, and practiced twice a day.

"We're doing Oklahoma Drill today fellas! Ever heard of that, Fendi?"

I hadn't.

Coach Levine dubbed it "a man's drill." It didn't seem too difficult from what was explained to me. Two guys line up in front of each other. The offensive player tries to block the defensive player from making a tackle on the running back.

Simple right?

"It's a one-on-one drill, and usually the highlight of practice!" Levine added.

I quickly learned this Oklahoma Drill separated the tough from the weak.

"You're going first, Fendi."

I didn't really know what to expect, but I had been doing a good job blocking thus far, so I was ready to try it. I wasn't too worried about it.

From my improvement in camp Levine bumped me up with the first group. I was now getting reps with the 1's. I was moving up.

A lot was being thrown at me, but I welcomed it. Levine remained patient with my development because I was showing signs of improvement everyday.

"Good catch, Fendi!" Levine yelled as I caught a pass on a ten-yard out route. A couple of seconds later, I heard a long whistle blow from Coach Sumlin.

"Oklahoma Drill!" he screamed.

All the O-linemen, D-linemen, linebackers, and tight ends ran to the field where the drill was set up. Everyone was fired up. There were four different stations. I walked up to mine, which was furthest to the left.

Each station had a little lane for the ball carrier to run behind the offensive blocker. The lane was pretty small. The drill started furthest from the right, so I got a chance to watch a few reps before it was my turn. The running back couldn't shift to the right or left because the lane was so narrow. The block had to be made in order for the ball carrier to go through.

Everybody was screaming, chanting, and yelling as the players crashed into each other. It was definitely a high-impact drill.

I was up, and I had no idea who was in front of me: I just knew he was a linebacker with 30 on his jersey.

He stood in a two-point stance; I was in a three. The O-line coach briefly explained what was going on, but there was so much commotion, I couldn't hear what he was saying.

I didn't know when my cue was to go. I wasn't sure if it was on the quarterback, or the snap of the ball. I had to hurry and get in my stance. All I knew was I had block the guy in front of me. I just didn't know when.

I could feel the anticipation getting higher, then it got quiet. Real quiet.

"Go! Hit!"

I lunged out to the backer, and shot my hands to make the block. I had just about reached him—

BOOM!!

The top of his helmet came directly under the screws of my helmet. Number 30 completely knocked my center of my gravity backwards. I flew three yards back to the ground, then he flipped the running back in the air with another hard hit.

"OH-H-H-H!"

A roar came from the sidelines. I was in a daze. That linebacker rang my bell. Matter of fact, he made a highlight out of me, flat out. There was nothing I could do but get up and take the humiliation.

I heard the laughs, and it was embarrassing. The equivalent of what just took place was a body-to-body dunk, *and one*. That was the magnitude of 30's hit. It was that bad, and I knew it.

The D-line coach was so excited he made a bee-line to me from the other side of the field just to say, "How you like that, basketball player!?"

He had it out for me: I had been killing his defensive ends all camp.

I later learned that the linebacker was Matt Nicholson, redshirt senior and the team's hardest hitter. He had also been one of the tackle leaders the year before.

I was set up.

The staff knew what they were doing when they put me against him. I had no clue, and Matt had no problem welcoming me to football through Oklahoma Drill.

I had to redeem myself. *Now* I knew what to expect. I was ready to go at it again. After a few reps, it was my turn again. This time it wasn't against Matt. Go figure.

I lined up better prepared this time.

"Go! Hit!"

Boom!

I came off the ball better and was able to make the block. It wasn't pretty, but it was better than my first try. It wouldn't cover up the highlight that was previously made of me, but I showed I could take a hit and get back up.

One bad block wasn't going to scare me away. The next drill was inside zone, a blocking drill where the O-line and the D-line go against each other simulating run plays. Since we were in full pads, this was another live drill.

"Go! Hit!"

Pow!

I heard my pads thud against the defender's, and my helmet popped his helmet back.

I came off the ball low and aggressive. I made the block and created a hole.

"*Good, Fendi*!" I heard Coach Levine scream. I knew I had made a good block. I was still fuming from Oklahoma Drill. I wasn't about to be clowned again.

A couple of reps later, I was up for another round. I was on the right side, and the play was going to the left. I had the backside cutoff block—my specialty. I was going against the defensive end I had been killing all camp. I was ready to expose him even more.

Waiting for the snap, I knew I was quicker than he was, so I had the advantage.

"Go! Hit!" The ball was snapped.

I took my first step with my left foot to cut him off, then my right foot followed. I had good position on him, but he was fighting to stop me from getting into his gap. While trying to stop me he tripped himself.

All 260 pounds of him crashed onto my right ankle.

My right leg went inward, and the defensive end fell right on it. The next thing I knew, I was on the ground, screeching in pain.

I knew it wasn't good; it *felt* like it was broken. I got up and limped to the trainer, so I knew my ankle wasn't broken, but it was the worst pain I had ever felt in my ankle. Ever.

I was helped onto the golf cart and taken to the training room. I was so angry. Just as things were getting better for me, this happens.

Had that clumsy D end kept his feet, my ankle wouldn't have been as big as a softball.

Right then, I realized why Coach Sumlin always yelled, "Stay off the ground!" during practice.

CHAPTER **14**
GROWING PAINS

I had suffered from ankle injuries before, but never one like this. When I got to the training room, the doctor looked at me and said it was a high ankle sprain.

"Typical football injury, Fendi," he said matter-of-factly.

Typical football injury maybe, but it wasn't so typical for me. My time was already limited, and this injury didn't help. I felt helpless.

I wanted to tell myself I'd be fine by the inter-squad scrimmage in a couple of days, but I knew I wouldn't be. I could barely walk.

I left the training room in a walking boot. Coach Levine called later that night to check on me. He asked how I was feeling.

"Disappointed," I told him. I was scheduled for an X-ray and an MRI the next morning.

I knew God had more for me. It couldn't end like this. I was just praying it wasn't serious.

I spent most of the next morning at the doctor's office doing tests and examinations. I was nervous from all the testing. I didn't know if I had a ligament tear or a fracture. I was hoping for the best news, but the worst possibilities kept going through my mind.

Hours later, the doctor called me with the results.

"Well, Fendi, the good news is I didn't find any breaks in any bones around the ankle area. However, you do have a medium-grade high ankle sprain that will take some time to heal."

"How long do you think I will be out for, Doc?" I asked, hoping it wouldn't be too long.

"Based on the grade of this injury, I'm thinking anywhere from six to eight weeks."

"Six to eight weeks, Doc?!" I almost cried. "You serious?"

My head dropped when he told me the news. I was dismayed about the situation. Then, I started realizing it could have been worse. I could have been done for the season or required surgery.

Despite the bad news, I had to find the light in the situation. At that point, it was hard. All I could do was thank God it wasn't worse.

I started planning immediately. The UH training room was going to be my second home. I had to ensure I did everything possible to get back on that field ASAP.

Looking at the time frame, best-case scenario was I would only miss the first game of the season. Perhaps it was a blessing in disguise, but I wanted to be out there competing for a spot.

Two-a-days were where the foundation was set, and I was missing it all. This program was what I *needed*. This was my last shot. I asked God why it had to go down like this.

Disappointed and angry, I knew I had to keep moving.

I kept telling myself it was temporary. There wasn't much I could do from a physical standpoint outside of rehab, so I used the extra time to become a film rat and really learn football.

Anytime I wasn't rehabbing, I was in the film room, studying the game, learning as much as I could about it. I was going to come back from this injury a better football player.

That weekend we had our first inter-squad scrimmage. The stands were full of fans. In the midst of the excitement I was void of emotion.

To add insult to injury, five NFL scouts approached me—five!

I had to tell them why I wasn't participating in the scrimmage. It was frustrating, extremely frustrating. I knew they were interested in seeing me play, and there I was stuck on the sidelines in a walking boot.

I saw Mr. Highsmith the Green Bay scout who had told me to use my fifth year to play football. He was at the scrimmage to watch me.

"Fendi, you hurt already? This ain't basketball, kiddo. How are we supposed to see you when you got a boot on your foot?"

He was right, but what could I do? I had to wait it out and hope to get some interest later when the season started.

On August 17, 2009, a few days later, Fox News blindsided me with an interview.

The NCAA had finally cleared waivers for me to use my 5th year of eligibility for football! After I got in the University and my grad program, I thought I was official, but I soon discovered there were still more regulations that had to be met before I could actually play. The NCAA had finally given me the OK to compete in games.

This was big. I started to see write-ups about the interview online—ESPN had it running on its college football channel—and I was getting calls from all over the country from reporters asking me about the transition.

The publicity was crazy.

The media was talking about players transitioning from collegiate basketball to collegiate football, and there were a couple guys doing the same thing. A point guard from Duke University was playing quarterback at Syracuse, and a power forward at Miami was also making the transition to the Canes football team as a tight end.

The basketball to football transition was a hot topic, and it attracted a lot of buzz. Unfortunately for me, the news from the NCAA and all the publicity didn't mean much.

I was still sidelined for another five weeks.

Two-a-days ended and classes started. I had actually forgotten about school during the chaos of two-a-days. I applied for financial aid to pay for school. It was my investment, my business decision.

I had the hopes I would be paid back tenfold in the NFL. Despite my injury, I had faith. My new dream was going to become a reality.

I started my master's program, and with my injury, I ended up spending more time in the classroom with classmates than I did with my teammates on the football field.

Three weeks had gone by, and my ankle was not progressing as fast as I would have liked. My ankle still throbbed every time I moved it. I knew high ankle sprains took time, but I was missing being on the field.

My days were so boring and monotonous without practice. I spent a lot of time with our head trainer Mike "Doc" O'Shea. Doc was well respected at the University. He had been UH's head trainer for about fifteen or so years. He had a sarcastic sense of humor. He didn't hold his tongue for anyone. You either hated him or you loved him. Everybody heard it from Doc. "Nobody is safe," was the word on Doc.

One day during rehab, he looked at me, perplexed, and said, "Fendi I have *no* clue how you're receiving all this attention from NFL scouts. You haven't done squat over here. I mean, they ask me questions I can't answer, because I haven't even seen you play before! You get blown up in Oklahoma Drill and hurt on day two of camp and people are tootin' *your* horn!?"

And he didn't stop there. "This has got to be a joke or something, right? I ain't tootin' nothing! But I *can* tell these scouts how Nicholson blew you up that one day in Oklahoma drill. That's all I've seen!"

Out of respect, I never said anything in response, and most of Doc's comments went in one ear and came out the other. But I didn't forget them. It was motivation. I was going to prove him wrong.

Doc always said, "I just call it like I see it," and I was going to show him something worth tootin' about.

Being with him was like watching a show. "Fendi, I bet you I'll become the president of the United States before you ever make it to the NFL!" And he was dead serious.

All I could do was laugh. "You better enter your name in the 2012 presidential election, because I'm goin,'" I shot back. "You'll see!"

Doc and I went at it daily. I could see why he'd give me heat though. I was completely new to football, and I was receiving a lot of NFL attention. I came in from nowhere, and I was getting calls.

I'm sure Doc didn't like that, but I didn't care. With Doc I had to always keep things in perspective. He was talking to scouts on my behalf, so I remained respectful. This was business, and this was my stepping stool to the NFL.

I wasn't going to let Doc's mouth or a high ankle sprain mess that up for me. I continued to learn the Cougar offense and the nuances of football from the film Coach Levine was giving me.

The days had crept by, and I was close to reaching the fifth week of my injury. I could tell my ankle was finally getting better, but it had not progressed to the point where I could practice.

Determined, I spent even more time in the training room. It felt like my ankle wouldn't heal any more quickly, no matter how much ice and therapy I did.

Five weeks felt like five months!

My dad reminded me to stay relentless. "Fendi, keep working hard in the training room. You have to stay diligent. You already know why you're here."

I had to make the most of it, no matter what cards I had been dealt.

The progression of my ankle finally allowed me to move to the next phase of rehab, a place called "muscle beach." Dreaded for the most part, muscle beach was like a slaughterhouse.

Far away, on a field of its own, it was the paradigm of a two-hour football boot camp. The sessions were brutal. Chad Dennis, the assistant strength and conditioning coach, ran it.

Dennis made guys magically heal faster, just so they wouldn't have to stay at the beach anymore; it had that type of effect.

My ankle wouldn't let me run or jump quite yet, so I couldn't do the conditioning. But I did all the calisthenics.

After a couple of days, I literally could not feel my arms or chest. My chest felt like it had been ripped open from the inside out because of all the pushups I had done. My conditioning was done in the water, because it took a lot of the pressure off my ankle.

While the others ran on land, I went to the underwater treadmill. After that I did thirty minutes of conditioning on the bike, then I would finish up on the jugs machine, catching 150 balls a day.

I was determined to get back to the field, and I stayed persistent. A week into my regimen my ankle got a lot stronger, and I was able jog on land. The improvement also meant I was at muscle beach full time.

Full-time muscle beach wasn't the greatest news, but I was relieved things were progressing.

CHAPTER 15
THE SEASON

I t was September, and the season was here. We were finally at week one, but I wouldn't be playing.

It had been seven weeks since the last time I practiced with the team. I felt like an afterthought—major MIA. I had tried to use this downtime as a learning experience and to get better mentally. It was all I could do.

Saturday was our first game, against Northwestern State. I walked into the locker room about twenty minutes before game time, and I encountered something I had never seen before.

The quiet demeanor of the team slowly turned as we got closer to game time. Guys started screaming at the top of their lungs and beating on lockers like maniacs. It was crazy in there. I wasn't sure if I was in a locker room or watching a WWE match.

"LET'S GO-O-O-O-O-O!"

This behavior was different from what I was accustomed to in basketball. The entire team was jacked. I felt like an outsider, a complete outsider. Our third-string quarterback came towards me with smelling salt in his hand and took a quick whiff of it.

"Woo-ho-o-o-o-o-o!" he screamed. "This ain't basketball, Fendi! It's a whole 'nother world! Who-o-o-o-o-o-o!"

A whole 'nother world, indeed.

As the season began, our team was finding new success. We killed Northwestern State and we beat fifth ranked Oklahoma State the following week. The upset made us the talk of the nation. No one had expected us to beat OSU.

We were rolling going into our bye week, and my ankle was feeling even better. I was at about eight weeks, and I was nearly running on land and able to make cuts. It felt great to be a little more mobile on the field, considering how long I was out, and the bye week was going to help tremendously.

Eight weeks is a long time. I had felt nearly invisible to the coaching staff during my rehab. Nobody talked to me. I learned quickly that when you're hurt in football, you're irrelevant. At least, it felt like that. I was eager to get back on the field and continue my development as a player.

I had a week and a half until the Texas Tech game. That was going to be my debut. All I had to do was pass my ankle examination and I would be cleared to play. My ankle was getting stronger, but I knew deep down I wasn't ready to come off the ball and block a defensive end.

I really couldn't cut or plant as well as I would have liked, but I could do it. I was probably 70%, but I was tired of sitting in the training room. My ankle felt decent enough, and I was going to play.

The week before the Tech game Coach Levine asked me how I felt.

"I feel good, Coach!"

"Good! We're going to use you as our jumper on field goal block and point after touchdown. Let's put some of those basketball skills to use!"

"Yes, sir!" I responded.

I was happy to get an opportunity to contribute. It was all I could ask for after being out for so long. Our offense was leading the country in passing yards, touchdowns, and points per game. We had the best offense in the country.

But there was a problem; we didn't use the tight end. We always lined up in four wide sets or five wide sets. We were running a spread offense. In the three games we had played, our offense had 250+ snaps. Of those snaps, the tight end was used in six of them. I was shocked.

Only six out of more than 250 snaps?

That was a problem. I didn't know if the low percentage tight-end use was due to *me* not being there, or if the Cougar offense really didn't utilize the tight end position. This was concerning.

The Texas Tech game was the biggest game of the year. It was a sold out game on ESPN. My excitement increased as game day got closer. Although I wasn't part of the game plan, I was *finally* suiting up and had a role on special teams. My ankle was about 80%.

I knew by Saturday, I'd be ready to go.

September 28, 2009. Game day.

All the bright lights were on. I hadn't seen anything like it before.

Coming from Tucson, I was used to seeing large crowds before basketball games. But from what I was told, that wasn't the norm here at UH. The band and cheerleaders met us off the bus as we walked to the locker room. We walked through the stadium to the school fight song, and all the fans cheered us on.

It was pretty cool. I was starting to notice the small differences between the two sports. The preparation was different, the approach was different, and it was a different mentality. Basketball would always have my heart, but football was beginning to grow on me.

We got to the locker room, and I looked around for my locker. I saw a sign that said "Tight Ends." There my uniform was, a couple feet away from me, folded in a cubby.

My first college football game: who would have thought?

We had fifty-five minutes until warm-ups, so I had to hurry to get taped and dressed.

Our game jersey had a tighter fit than our practice jerseys. I was wondering how I was going to put it over my shoulder pads. I grabbed my shoulder pads first and put them on.

"Wait, bro, you might want put the jersey on the pads first before you put 'em on," a teammate mentioned. "Trust me, it'll save you hassle and time."

I couldn't imagine how crazy I would have looked attempting to put that jersey over my pads *after* they were already on my shoulders—that would have been a show.

"Thanks, bro! I appreciate that!" I laughed to myself and continued to get ready for the game.

I didn't see too many guys wearing their lower pads, but I made sure I wore everything. I wanted to be protected!

I even wore my basketball knee sleeve. Why? I don't know; I just did. I felt like I was holding onto a piece of my first love. I held onto what I could.

I slid my knee sleeve on and pulled up my shiny white game pants. At Arizona, I always wore two pairs of socks for games and a knee sleeve. I did the same at Houston.

Now I almost felt like a true football player, but I was missing the finishing touch.

Watching the countless hours of college football on ESPN during my rehab, I always saw players with armbands and eye black. Some guys even wrote messages on their eye black. It looked cool.

"Five minutes until offense goes out"

I rushed to the back of the equipment room to grab a silver permanent marker. I owed this opportunity to my Lord and Savior Jesus Christ. He had made this all possible, and I was truly grateful to be in this moment.

In reverence, I abbreviated my favorite scripture on my patches: Colossians 3:23. My right patch read "COL" and my left one read "3:23." I put the patches under my eyes, and I was set.

Fully dressed and ready to go, I looked *huge*! I couldn't believe it. I couldn't wait to step foot on the field.

It was time for my coming out party.

Exiting the tunnel, I could see the bright lights. The field was lit up. Music was playing through the loud speaker, and it was an ESPN Saturday night game.

First collegiate football game.
September 28, 2009. *Photo courtesy of University of Houston Athletics*

My adrenaline was pumping. Running never felt so good. The atmosphere made me forget all about my ankle pain; I was in the zone.

The pregame clock was winding down, and the stage was set. This was a feeling I had never experienced before. Thirty-five thousand fans screaming and the band playing our fight song literally gave me chills. It was so much fun, and the game hadn't even started yet.

We scored on our first drive and took a quick 7-0 lead. Tech scored shortly after.

"PAT block! PAT block!" Levine yelled.

That was my cue. My heart was racing with anticipation as I ran on the field. The crowd sounded like thunder, they were so loud. I got in position, ready to jump as high as I could to block the kick.

The ball was snapped, and I jumped as high as I could. The referee signaled good kick. That was it! All of maybe seven seconds. I didn't know how close I was to the ball, it happened so fast.

"You were close, 81! Keep jumping!"

I had three more opportunities, but still no block. I couldn't get my hand near the ball. I had been jumping my entire career before football, but I didn't realize how hard it was to actually block a kick.

On the sidelines, I was trying to follow the game. Flags were being thrown all over the place, and I was still unsure what the calls were. I didn't fully understand everything going on, but I was still having fun playing my new sport.

We rallied and had some good drives in the fourth quarter to beat Texas Tech 29-28. It was a huge win for us. The students rushed the field at the end of the game. I had never been in anything like it.

Me in action with the PAT (Point After Touchdown) Block Unit. *Photo courtesy of University of Houston Athletics. Photo credit: Ashley Yarber*

What a game!

This was something I could definitely get used to. UTEP was on the schedule next, and the game was in El Paso, four hours away from Arizona. Keith and Billy were coming to watch. They were the ones who had ignited the football idea in the first place. It was only right to have them watch me on the gridiron.

We had another week planning and had to prepare for the Miners. From watching hours of film on their defense, I was picking up things a little better, but I was still cloudy on different coverage schemes.

I was trying my best to understand and follow everything, but everyone was moving so fast! I was just getting the offensive side of the ball down, along with defensive fronts, but coverage was another story. I didn't quite have that down yet.

Levine gave us the play script for UTEP. I highlighted every play that included my package. Of the 60 plays on the script, there were only three. Three plays, and they were runs. I didn't have anything else in the game plan.

My excitement and anticipation dropped. I had thought since I was a little healthier I'd play more. I didn't even want to travel west anymore.

I wanted my people from AZ to see me *play*.

CHAPTER 16

PRACTICING PATIENCE

We left for UTEP, and all I could think about on the flight there was how my people from Arizona were coming to watch me stand on the sidelines. I knew the chances of seeing the field on this one were slim.

Keith and Billy drove in from Tucson and paid me a visit at the hotel. It was their first time seeing me since I left for Houston.

"*Da-a-a-ng*!" yelled Billy. "You've been on them weights!"

"Look at your traps, Fendi! Jeez! What are you on, steroids?" Keith jokingly added.

"Can you believe you're here? You're on a football team! How do you like it? Do you miss basketball?" They were shooting question after question.

I tried to answer as best I could. It was complicated. "I'm having fun. It's different. But fun." I gave them a half smile.

"I can't believe we're actually here to watch you play football."

"I'm not playing," I told them flatly.

"Fendi, you're part of the team. You're practicing and getting better, and you *will* play. It's unbelievable just from the perspective of how far you've come. I'm so proud of you man. This is amazing!" Keith was all smiles. "The plan is still intact!" he added.

"This will be a great learning tool for you, Fendi, whether you play or not. Soak it up and get better. This is what the scouts said you needed last year. Keep your head up," Billy told me.

We had meetings, so I had to leave, but I continued to hold on to what Keith and Billy told me. I had come a long way. I needed to stay positive and keep reminding myself it was all part of the plan.

Patience is a virtue.

We lost the game to UTEP, and I still hadn't touched the ball in a game. I was doing some blocking, but it wasn't much.

I continued to make the most out of practice. That was where I was going to show the coaches I wanted to play. I was getting more comfortable as a football player. My practice habits and techniques were getting better. I could feel myself becoming more and more familiar with the game.

At position meetings that week, Levine walked into the room.

"Fendi, we got Tulane next week, and the way they play, we'll need to use you. I guarantee you will play more on offense, so just be ready! Mark my words! *This* week we have a fake installed on field goal. You might get your first touchdown against Mississippi State!

"You'll be on the left side, and all you have to do is block the rush defense. I'll show you the technique later. If we go with the fake, you'll hear the cue and run to the back left pylon for the score."

Okay, simple enough.

Thinking about my first touchdown, I played the fake out in my mind all throughout the meeting. During practice, Coach Sumlin and Coach Levine taught me the technique. We practiced the block and the fake a few times a day. It definitely felt good catching the football.

I was ready for my first score.

On game day, we made our way to Davis Wade stadium. I knew I was going to play. I could slowly see the coaching staff working me in. I was hoping for the fake to be called, but it all depended on the "look."

The game went well. I played my part on PAT/FG block, but we never got an opportunity to run the fake. I thought it was there, but Levine said it wasn't.

I wanted that touchdown so bad. Even if the look wasn't there, I just wanted to score. We got out of Starksville with a 31-24 victory and were now 4-1, but our recent loss at UTEP knocked us out of the top 25.

Week seven was here, and Tulane was up. This was the week Levine said I'd play, and it was about time! I really wanted to play. I was anxious to see if I was in this week's game plan.

During the meeting, Coach passed out the plan. As always, I searched for my formations. I was happily surprised to see there were quite a few formations for twelve personnel. Levine was right: I was *actually* going to play.

"I see I got work this week, Coach."

"I know!" Levine replied. "Let's see what you're going to do with it."

My ankle was stronger than ever, and I was ready to contribute to the offense. It was going to be a good week.

During practices, I was getting reps with the first team offense. I even had a goal line touchdown play! Saturday couldn't come quick enough.

Tulane had a defensive end that Levine was hyping up all week. He didn't look all that good on film. I was going to destroy him. I couldn't wait for the challenge.

We got to the Mercedes Benz Superdome that Saturday morning. I didn't know if it was a sign from God or another one of His humorous acts, but the irony of playing my first real football game in an NFL stadium was not lost on me.

"It's time to make your money, 81, this is what you've been waiting for!" Juice said.

Juice was right; I had been waiting for this. The opportunity had *finally* come.

"You ready, Onobun? Are you ready?" Levine asked.

I looked in his eyes and nodded. *I'm ready.*

I had no words for him—I was ready to play.

The game was sluggish from start. By the end of the first half we were up 9 – 6, and I still hadn't gotten in. I watched the slow paced game from the sidelines, impatiently waiting to hear my formation.

Two drives later, we were approaching the goal line. "Deuce, Deuce, Deuce!" Coach Holgorsen yelled out.

I sprinted onto the field, calling the formation. We were three yards away from the end zone, and a touchdown would put us up 23-6.

I was more than ready. I approached the line of scrimmage and got in my stance.

"515, 515!" Case yelled, "Go-o-o-o, hit!"

I attacked the defender in front of me and got a good push off the ball.

As I shot my hands towards his shoulder pads, I literally bench pressed him backwards off the line of scrimmage. The block created a hole for the running back, and he scored; it was perfect!

"*Touchdown Cougars!*"

I heard it over the loudspeaker! I was more excited than the running back who actually scored! I felt like I had scored!

"Great block, Fendi! Great block down there!" the OC said.

That play developed the coordinator's trust in me. Coach Holgorsen saw that I could go out and make a play like I had been there before. More plays started coming my way.

Going into the fourth quarter, I got a chance to play more since we ran the ball so much to eat up the clock. Throughout the game, I was getting more comfortable and confident on the field.

We drove the ball again to the goal line. The OC looked at me. "You ready to make a play?"

I looked at him and said confidently, "Let's do it!"

"All right, go get one!"

Holgorsen called out my formation to the field. I knew exactly what the play was. *This one was for me.*

As I ran to the goal line in excitement, all I could think to myself was *Touchdown, Touchdown, Touchdown*. I had been practicing it all week: "Pop 24."

Case was going to throw it up for me to go get it in the back of the end zone. We had been over it so many times. I was ready for it.

I listened for Case on the cadence. The defense was set up perfectly. "Go-o-o-o-o-o-hit!"

I got off the line and ran to the linebacker as if I was going to block him. He froze waiting on my move, I pushed him aside and got to the back of the end zone. I looked up and the ball was already in the air. I jumped off my back right foot as high as I could with two hands in the air to catch the ball.

Just before I could fully extend, I was knocked down in mid air and clipped to the ground. I landed on my back. That was my chance. Gone.

Dang it! I slapped the turf in frustration

To my surprise my teammates were clapping and cheering. "They threw a flag!" I heard someone say.

"P.I.! P.I.!"

I got up, and Case came to me.

"Hey, it was a pass interference on the defense, that's good!" he said, slapping me on the back. "C'mon, we'll get it next time."

"Oh, okay… good!" I still had no idea what technically happened. I didn't even know what pass interference was. I was more concerned that I hadn't caught my first touchdown opportunity.

We eventually ran the ball in for another score. It was a blowout, and I played a good part of the second half.

It felt good to finally contribute on the field.

CHAPTER **17**
SETTLING IN

The next week people began to treat me differently, especially the coaches. Those who hadn't said two words to me all season were speaking to me now.

"Hey, Fendi, how are you doing today?"

I kind of smirked to myself—*Oh, now you see me?*

"Doing well, Coach. How are you?"

Before that, I had never heard this one coach say my name. It was funny. You do a few things well, then all of sudden you're noticeable. Typical coaches.

We had SMU coming to us this week. Going through our normal routine, I watched film on the Mustangs' defense, preparing myself to play. I didn't know if I'd get another chance to play, but I sure hoped for it. The game against Tulane had been fun. It was great to *actually play.*

Tuesday afternoon fast approached. On the way to position meetings, I walked into our room looking for the week's script. My eyes raced through the game plan. I skimmed through forty calls before I saw the list of tight end sets.

Sweet! I'm playing again.

I even had a couple of pass plays on the list.

Now we're talkin'.

"Fendi, you got your work cut out for this Saturday," Levine said. "We need you to make a reach block on a wide run. This is a big-time block, and it's not easy!"

We had a reverse pitch play installed in the game plan. The play was coming to my side. I was going to have to make a huge reach block on the outside defender for the play to work.

"You might not be able to reach him, so just run him out of the way and create a hole," Coach told me.

"Why wouldn't I be able to reach him?" I asked.

"It's a tough block. You more than likely won't get square on him to reach; you'll just have to wash him out."

I didn't believe that one bit. Coach Levine didn't know how fast I was—*clearly.*

"I bet you I do get square and reach that outside block. Matter of fact I know I will. Just watch me on Saturday. I'm going to make that block."

I couldn't believe he told me I wouldn't be able to reach the block. I was going to prove him wrong.

Throughout the week we worked and perfected the script. There was a play action set where I was the first read. There wasn't a doubt in my mind I going to have my first catch against SMU.

I was way overdue.

Saturday night arrived, and it was show time! We were hosting the Mustangs, and it was an important game. We were tied in conference play. This game was the tiebreaker; it was going to be a war.

Deep down my confidence was high. *I am going to make my blocks, catch the ball, and play physical.* That was all there was to it.

My eye black patches read "Phil" and "4:13." *I can do all things through Christ who strengthens me.* I was going onto the battlefield not only with my own strength but also with God's.

Only thing left to do was play football.

We came out firing from the jump. I got a couple plays in during the first two quarters and made some good blocks. I was waiting for the play action and the reverse to be called

I knew the plays were coming soon. We built a good lead, and I wanted to prove Levine wrong. The score was 24-3 at the half.

We started the second half with a 92-yard return to push the score up 31-3. A couple of drives later, the OC yelled out my formation, "Slot, slot!"

I jetted to the field and got to my spot.

"518! 518!" Case yelled.

My reach block.

Every ounce in my body was determined to make this play.

"Go-o-o-o-o, hit!"

I took off running to my defender's outside shoulder. The further I reached the further he tried to stay outside. I had to reach him at a flat angle towards the sidelines to engage contact and make the block. He was already outside of me. I got my hands on him, and my speed helped me reach him.

I made the block.

"*Go-o-o-o-od!*" I heard Levine from the sidelines as I was making the block. He jumped up in excitement.

I reached the defender and got square on him. The block was *better* than it had been drawn.

Tyron was to my left on the reverse, and he zoomed past where the hole was created. It was 10-yard gain.

"First down!" the announcer said. The Cougars faithful went wild.

I *knew* I could make that block.

I ran back to the sidelines looking for Levine.

"Did you see that, Coach? Did you see that? I reached him! I told you I would!"

I was hyped! I knew I had it all along.

We were moving the chains, and I was listening to every formation being called. The ball was on our 43 and I heard, "Deuce, Deuce!"

I had to hold my excitement because I knew what play was coming, and I was about to catch this ball. I got to the line of scrimmage, and Case signaled the play.

"515 Playboy! 515 Playboy! Go-o-o-o-o, Hit!"

I shot out of my stance like a cannon and sold the backside block on the defensive end. Case faked the handoff to the left and rolled back to my side. I got off my block and ran towards the sideline—it was a classic naked bootleg.

I saw Case's eyes looking right at me. The ball was coming my way. My eyes widened; I watched it softly spiral into my hands, and I tucked it as if I had been doing it for years.

Once I caught that ball, it felt like everything was in slow motion.

All I saw was green grass. I didn't see anyone or anything else. I was just running.

"*Go! Go! Go!* " I could hear my teammates on the sidelines. Each step I took hit with more and more force. I was gaining momentum and running faster, in full stride. I still didn't see anyone. My eyes were on the end zone.

Boom!

I was flipped. My legs were taken from under me on the tackle; all I could think was *Hold on to the ball!*

I landed and popped up in excitement.

"Pass completed to Fendi Onobun on the catch, for another Cougar First Down!"

First catch! October 24, 2009 at Robertson Stadium, Houston, Texas. *Nick de la Torre /* © *Houston Chronicle. Used with permission. Photo courtesy of The Houston Chronicle.*

I took off to the sidelines overjoyed. It was such a surreal feeling. I didn't even know what was really going around me: I was in the moment. I had just made my first catch.

Everyone was buzzing.

"I see you Fendi!"

"Good job 81!"

"Yeah boy! Nice catch!"

Then Coach Sumlin congratulated me. "Good job, son," and Holgorsen gave me a tap to the helmet. Everyone on the team knew how truly special that moment was for me.

I was so overwhelmed with the play I had to snap back into the game

"Hey, 81, nice catch, but you have a game to get back to!" It was Levine. The game wasn't over.

The fourth quarter went by fast, and the final score was 38-15. We were 6-1 overall and 2-1 in conference play. My role was increasing, and I was contributing to the wins. It felt good.

I was finding my place and settling in. This was just the beginning.

I couldn't wait to see how I would evolve.

Dee and I were going into our fifth move. A week after we settled back into the motel, Dee found a family for us to move in with—the family of her co-worker. They were a very sweet white family, and they had a dog.

It was a little weird, but they were nice. It wasn't as bad as the last guy's place, and it smelled better than the motel.

I felt adopted. We had a place to stay for a few weeks until we finally got a place of our own.

"It's going to be just me and you soon, Poops," Dee would say.

Her statement scared me, but I'd rather be with my mom than some strangers.

Weeks passed, and, just as planned, we were able to move into a place of our own. It was a small, furnished apartment.

"Don't forget your Nintendo, Poops," Dee said.

I grabbed it along with my bag of toys. Walking up the stairs of our new apartment home, I was feeling better.

I still missed my dad, and I missed Houston, but this place was better than the last six places we had lived.

The whole time I had been in Las Vegas, any time I was alone with a phone, I always tried to call home. But I could never get through. My hope was that my dad would find me one day because I missed him so much. I missed my school too.

There was no school for me here in Vegas, so I watched *The Price Is Right* and ate Spaghetti-O's and corn pops with my nanny everyday until Dee got home. I had my bag of toys and my video game.

This was the best it had been for me since we got here. I was getting somewhat comfortable and more relaxed now that we finally had a clean place of our own.

We had to get ready for week nine, and our squad was rolling. Southern Miss was the next victim. After Monday meetings, Coach Levine pulled me to the side.

"Meet me in my office, will ya? Somebody wants to meet ya." He didn't explain.

"All right Coach, I'll be right up there." I went to my locker and grabbed my things, wondering who it could be.

When I got to Levine's office and knocked on the door, he opened it. There was another gentleman sitting in the office watching film—of me!

"Fendi, I wanted to introduce you to this scout from the Chicago Bears," Levine said calmly.

The orange 'C' on his navy blue shirt was the *first* thing I noticed. I extended my hand and introduced myself. I had the biggest smile on my face.

"Fendi! Pleasure to meet you!" he said warmly.

"Pleasure to meet you too, sir!" I replied.

We spoke briefly about my transition and how the season was going for me thus far. I couldn't believe I was talking to a scout from the Chicago Bears! I knew I was doing something right.

"Well, keep at it," the scout said. "You have great potential."

"Thank you, sir," I said, shaking his hand.

"Alright, Fendi, I'll see tomorrow in meetings," said Levine.

"Alright, Coach!"

I had a plan when I came here, and it was still about that. I had to keep improving and learning the game. My goal was to be an NFL-ready tight end by the time my year was up, and I was going to keep working towards that.

But this week the focus was Southern Miss.

A couple of scouts came to practice on Thursday, one from the Baltimore Ravens and another from the Jacksonville Jaguars. Levine was a little tougher than usual on me.

"Come off the ball!"

"Stay low, Fendi!"

"Drive your feet!"

"Burst after the catch!"

All I heard was Levine's mouth that practice.

I had two NFL scouts watching my every move, but Levine's hard coaching didn't bother me—if anything it made me practice harder. I knew I was getting better and it was important that I had a good practice in front of those scouts.

I did a lot of blocking and extra route running afterwards, since I didn't get too many opportunities to catch during practice. Overall, it was one of my more productive days.

"Good practice, Fendi. You know, if you practice like that everyday, everything else will take care of itself—scouts and everything we've talked about," Coach Levine told me. "You definitely got better today."

In field goal and PAT block meetings, Levine told me Southern Miss' kicker had been struggling the past two weeks. "So you might get a block this Saturday." Levine was a mastermind when it came to special teams. He would come up with schemes and plays that made our unit one of the best in the conference.

It was Halloween morning, and we were getting ready to play against the Golden Eagles. During our special teams meetings that morning, we were watching film on their kicker. Looking at his kicks from the previous week, we could clearly see the flight of his kicks. Levine pointed out the trajectory of it with his laser pen. "You see how low that is?"

I had yet to block a kick, and it was getting a little frustrating; I never realized how hard they were to block.

"Fendi, I guarantee you, absolutely guarantee you, you'll get a block today. One of y'all will. This kicker kicks low."

Levine would sometimes put in two jumpers to block kicks, depending on the team we were playing. Today was one of those days.

We were ranked 18th on the BCS Poll coming into this game, and it wasn't going to be a cakewalk; we had to come out ready. We fumbled the ball on our first drive, and Southern Miss took advantage. They scored, making it 6-0 them.

"PAT block PAT block!" Levine yelled.

I buckled up my helmet and got to my spot. The other jumper and I lined up right above the snapper, ready for the kick. The ball was snapped.

I timed my jump just as the kicker approached the ball.

POP!

Blocked kick! Me (right) blocking Southern Miss' PAT kick at Robertson Stadium, Houston, Texas. October 31, 2009

The ball hit my hand and plopped over the ground. Everything happened so quickly I almost didn't see it. Our corner picked it up and started running it back toward our end before he got tackled.

"Ah-h-h-h-h!" I screamed in joy. My first block! I ran back to the sidelines after the play, I was showered with high fives and helmet taps.

"Nice block, Fen!"

"Good job, 81!"

"You were up there man!"

"Good play!"

The block helped us get ahead by the end of the first quarter. The scoreboard read 7-6, us.

I got a few plays in during the second quarter and made some blocks; I also had my first error and messed up one of the blocking calls.

I was still hyped about my PAT block, and my mind just went blank at the line.

"Go-o-o-o-o, Hit!" That was all I heard, and I didn't know the call. I had to get my hands on someone and make a block. They play was broken up by the Golden Eagles defense.

"What was your call?" Levine said.

"Fourteen?" I guessed.

"NO! C'mon, son!" he reprimanded me. "Tyler! Make sure he hears and knows the call."

Levine walked away.

"My mistake. I drew a blank man," I told Tyler, the other tight end. "What was the call?"

"Truck," he said.

"Dang. That was my solo block on the defensive end."

"Yep, I was wondering what you were doing," said Tyler.

I didn't know why I spaced out on the field. But I knew I had to make up for it fast, I couldn't let it worry me; there was still more football to play.

At the end of the first it was 13-7 Southern Miss.

In the second quarter, we had to step it up. We scored on our first drive, putting us in the lead. It was a shootout. The Golden Eagles responded making the score 21-19, us.

"PAT block! PAT block!"

I buckled up my helmet and ran onto the field. The kicker took his approach, and I timed his step perfectly for my jump.

Pop! Blocked again!

I saw the ball all the way into my hands this time; it ricocheted off my fingertips and bounced toward our safety. He grabbed it and took off running towards our end zone. I ran as fast as I could, following him for blocks.

He found a hole and took it to the house. Ninety-five yards later the score was 23-19. That was my second block in the game! I couldn't believe it!

"YEA-A-A-A-H! LET'S GO!"

Despite the blocked kicks, the game remained close all the way through; we scored, then they would score. It was back and forth.

We ended up winning the game 50-43, and our record was now 7-1.

Someone pointed out to me that had I not made those two blocks, we would have lost by two. It showed me how crucial those blocks really were.

"Yeah, baby! 7 and 1! 7 and 1, yea-a-a-h!" Everyone was chanting the new record in the locker room. It was a tough game, but we had pulled it through. We were playing good football.

My blocked kicks made ESPN Sports Center. I was the conference special teams player of the week, and I was really starting to like this transition.

It looked like my business decision was paying off. Things were beginning to look up for me—finally.

We had Tulsa up next, and we knew it was going to be another tough one. We were able to rally and beat the Golden Hurricanes with a last-second field goal, making us now 8-1.

We had three games left in the season: Central Florida, Memphis, and Rice.

Central Florida was leading CUSA East, and we were leading CUSA West. It was a showdown when we played them.

We got off to a good start, but UCF handed us our second lost of the season. We lost 37-32, and I didn't play a single snap.

I had felt that things were beginning to look up for me and that I was growing as a football player, then all of a sudden I didn't play.

At Houston, we ran a spread offense that didn't involve the tight end very much. But hindsight is always 20/20.

Despite my confusion, I knew I couldn't let any negative feelings linger. I was still on a mission whether they used the tight end or not.

We had to get ready for Memphis. I hadn't been involved with the offense much since the Tulane game, but my package was up this week. I was ready for my number to be called.

Memphis came into town, and we jumped on them quick with a 21-7 lead by the end of the first quarter. I got two penalties on field goal moving before the snap of the ball. It caused us 10 yards in penalties.

Then, in the second quarter, I dropped a pass from Case in the Red Zone.

Talk about pissed.

I couldn't believe it. I had practiced the route all week, and I hadn't dropped a single ball. It hit me right in the numbers and bounced off my chest. I was fuming.

After the play, Coach Sumlin pulled me to the side and told me to calm down, have fun, and play like was capable of playing.

We were up 42-14 at the half, and I had to calm myself down during the break. I was still angry at myself. I took my phone and wrote a quick note. I read it over and over again.

"Fendi, calm down! You can do this, God wouldn't put you through a situation you couldn't handle, relax, have fun, and play football!

BE CONFIDENT IN YOURSELF, CATCH THE FOOTBALL FIRST, LOOK IT IN, CATCH THE BALL AND TUCK IT.

Houston vs. Memphis at Robertson Stadium, November 21, 2009, Houston, Texas. *Photo courtesy of University of Houston Athletics*

CATCH THE BALL FENDI YOU CAN DO THIS! LOOK IT IN, CATCH THE BALL!

You can do it Fen, you can do it, God is with you, and he is your only audience, HE IS WHO YOU ARE PLAYING FOR, AUDIENCE OF ONE, HE'S GOT U."

I read those words over and over and again.

They reminded me who I was playing for, and who was in control. That was my peace.

I knew what I was capable of. If I played hard with confidence in myself, I knew everything would take care of itself.

Jogging back to the field after halftime, I was ready to go back and play. Memphis started the second half with the ball and turned it over on downs. We replied with another score, putting us up 35 with 12 minutes left in the third quarter.

Memphis couldn't respond; we were thrashing them.

"Deuce! Deuce!"

I sprinted on the field and got to my spot. Our second-string QB, Cotton Turner, gave the signal, tapping his boot. This was the exact same play we ran earlier when I dropped the ball.

I was determined to catch it this time.

"Go-o-o-o-o-o, Hit"

I came off the ball clean past the defensive end and ran under the strong-side linebacker to my depth. I was behind the middle linebacker, as he couldn't catch me on the run. I was sprinting across the field, open.

Cotton saw me open and led me perfect with the ball. I plucked it out the in stride. As soon as the ball hit my hands, I tucked it and bolted towards the end zone.

Two steps and a dive later—*TOUCHDOWN COUGARS!*

I had just scored my first touchdown!

I heard the horns, and I couldn't believe it. I celebrated with my teammates and capped off the game with that score. I was ecstatic; and made up for my drop earlier.

Teammates greeted me with high fives and helmet taps on the sideline.

"Nice catch, 81!"

"First touchdown, Fendi! Good job!"

"Longtime coming!" Levine said, grinning from ear to ear.

First Touchdown! Houston vs. Memphis at Robertson Stadium, November 21, 2009, Houston, Texas. *Photo courtesy of University of Houston Athletics*

I had been waiting for this moment, and it had finally come. We ended up beating Memphis 55-14, and I had finally scored a touchdown.

It was definitely a good day, and I couldn't do anything but thank God. The letter I wrote to myself during halftime had helped. As upset as I was, I was able to go to God and clear my head. I had peace and I was confident. He took care of the rest. I knew once I refocused, He would carry me through.

Week thirteen was here, and it was the last game of the regular season. We had already clinched the

Celebrating 6 with my teammates after scoring my first TD! vs Memphis November 21st, 2009 Robertson Stadium, Houston, Texas. *Photo courtesy of University of Houston Athletics*

CUSA West title, and a win against our cross-town rival Rice would only make it that much better.

This game was known as the "Bayou Bucket," and after last season's loss, the bucket wasn't in our trophy case.

I didn't know much about the rivalry, but it didn't take a rocket scientist to know these two schools didn't like each other. The previous year Rice had torched UH, and it was time for revenge.

The goal this week was to "Get The Bucket Back." Rice was coming into our home stadium 2-10. We knew, record aside, they were going to give us their best shot.

And we were going to do the same.

Throughout the week of practice, I saw more scouts trickle in sporadically. I was the only senior on the team receiving NFL attention, so I felt like they were here to see me. My inactivity during practices became wearisome.

It was frustrating. This was my only opportunity to get to the next level. I wanted to do so much more, and my time was running out.

One day that week, there was a scout from the Carolina Panthers at our practice. Our receivers were working on routes on air. The tight ends weren't a part of the drill.

The drill was for our receivers, but the scout wanted to see me. Coach Levine told me to get in line and run a route after about five minutes. I knew what he was trying to do. But it was still frustrating.

The tight end was an afterthought in this offense, but all I could do was make the best of it. God had a plan, and man wasn't going to hold me back.

It was our last game of the season, and we wanted to cap it off with a win. I had a goal line touchdown play in the game plan, and I was hungry for another one.

With the bucket on the line, we came out firing. Twenty seconds into the game, Tyron had an 80-yard kickoff return, making it 7-0, us. Rice had a hard time taming us, and I was playing more than I had all season.

Rice's defensive end was giving me a hard time. He was shedding all my blocks and making tackles off them.

"C'MON. FENDI! HE'S KILLING YOU! MAKE YOUR BLOCK!" Levine yelled.

The next play I was flagged for a holding call. I didn't know how this guy was shedding my blocks.

"Flag on the play; holding offense 81. Ten-yard penalty!"

"C'MON FEN!" I yelled to myself.

This was the most I had played in a game all year, and I was getting exposed. I had to fix it fast.

"You've got to drive your feet on the block, Fendi. You're not moving your feet to keep momentum," I heard Coach Dennis telling me.

Our assistant strength coach from Muscle Beach had been watching me the entire drive and was able to see why I was struggling with the Rice defensive end. He went on, "Yeah, Fendi, he's shedding your blocks because you're not driving him back. Stay low and move your feet."

I had been beaten three times. I had to stay on my block and stop him.

Drinking from "The Bucket" after defeating Rice in The Bayou Bucket Game November 29, 2009 at Robertson Stadium, Houston, Texas.

Our offense was driving the ball down the field, and we got all the way to the five-yard line.

"DEUCE, DEUCE!"

I knew it was my touchdown play. I lined up and surveyed the defense. The defensive end was to my inside and the linebacker was to my right. The safeties were up close. Case gave me the signal.

"514! 514! Go-o-o-o-o, Hit!"

I came off the ball and ran my pop route towards the goal post, looking for the lob. The safeties were zoned in and the defensive line blitzed. Case started to scramble; I was running in the same direction at the back of the end zone looking for the ball.

Throw it! Throw it!

Case tucked it and ran it in for the score.

"TOUCHDOWN COUGARS!"

The fans erupted! I was the first one to celebrate with Case in the end zone. I was glad we had gotten the score, but I wanted that ball; I wanted that touchdown.

We were up 14-0. Coach Dennis kept an eye on me throughout the game. His advice was helping me, and my blocks got better. Once I finally understood what I was doing wrong, I started driving my feet. The defensive end didn't make another tackle off me the entire game.

We were too much for the Owls. The final score was 73-14, and we got the bucket back!

We finished the regular season 10-2 and were the CUSA West champions.

I definitely grew and learned a lot in the Rice game. I had to deal with some adversity, and Levine wanted to see how I'd respond to it.

It was safe to say I was no longer a basketball player playing football; I had blossomed into a football player.

Our next challenge was the conference championship game against East Carolina (ECU) in Greenville, North Carolina, their home stadium. We knew it was going to be a tough game; our counterparts from the East had given us a hard time this year. We had marginal room for error.

Rice had given us confidence, but make no mistake: East Carolina was no Rice. The winner would advance to the Auto Zone Liberty Bowl, and that was our goal.

The week was a quick turnaround, as we had to get ready for an early Saturday morning championship game. For whatever reason, I didn't have many reps in practice. I really wasn't a part of the game plan.

Sometimes I played, and sometimes I didn't. I couldn't really see a pattern that explained why. The situation was frustrating, and it reminded me of my days at Arizona.

How will scouts see me play, if I'm not in the game?

I kept thinking, "My time is limited, man! It's almost over."

We got to Dowdy-Ficklin Stadium that Saturday morning, and it was full of people in purple and gold. This was basically a home game for ECU. I knew I wouldn't play much, but I was still excited. We had a chance to win the "Conference Ship." And that was the goal.

We started strong. ECU was having difficulty with our passing attack, and we had a 5-point lead by the end of the half. In the third quarter, we continued to make plays through the air, and ECU made theirs on the ground.

Our lead wasn't comfortable, but it was a lead. We had to keep playing good football. It was a grind-it-out type of game.

The momentum shifted in the second half after ECU capitalized on a few of our costly mistakes.

I couldn't get my hands on any kicks, either. Their kicker was completing everything!

By the end of the third, they scored 10 points, and it was 24-19, them. We came back in the fourth quarter and managed to score 13 more points to ECU's 14.

Down 6, our defense made a stop and gave us a chance to put together one last winning drive. With about a minute remaining, we took a shot on first down, but the ball was intercepted.

Just like that the game was over.

ECU won 38-32. Conference USA champions were on their way to the Liberty Bowl. I was sick to my stomach; we were so close, and we let it get away. That one hurt.

Nonetheless, we were still going to a bowl game. The rumor was we'd be going to the same bowl as the team had the year before: The Bell Helicopter Armed Forces Bowl.

There were a lot of mixed feelings about it. Last year's team finished 7-5, and this year we were 10-3. Going to the same bowl game gave us the feeling that we weren't any better than the year before, when actually we were. I had never been to a bowl game, so I was looking forward to it; but I understood the viewpoint of some of my teammates.

When the bowl games were officially announced, the rumor was proved right. We were headed to the Bell Helicopter Armed Forces Bowl. Not only was it the same bowl, it was also the exact same matchup from last year.

We had almost two weeks to prepare for the game. With the extended time the younger guys got more reps in practice until it was time to game plan for the opponent. The starters and rotational players would rest. I wasn't a younger player but I got extra reps too. Levine continued to be true to his promise and coached me up every single day, and I continued to grow and learn.

I wasn't the same player that I had been in August. My whole vibe was different now. I was consistently more comfortable as a football player.

I could tell I was different. I saw it in my attitude and the way I interacted with the guys. I understood more on the field, and practice got easier for me. I was doing so much better, and I was correcting my mistakes. I was getting more comfortable blocking, and my football terminology was growing. I just *felt* it.

We were a few days from our bowl game in Ft. Worth, and Levine broke the news to me: "Fendi, you're starting against Air Force."

"Really?!"

"Yep! We're starting the game out of Deuce. Be ready!"

I was making my first career start! Talk about growth.

December 31st, twelve noon. Air Force won the coin toss and elected to receive. They wanted revenge on their loss the year before. They jumped out to a quick 7-0 lead. Now it was our turn to respond.

"Deuce! Deuce!"

Coming out onto the field with 40,000 fans screaming was mesmerizing for me. I was starting! I knew what we were running, and I knew I was going to have to reach the outside backer who was wide to my right.

"518!! 518!! Go-o-o-o-o, Hit!"

I came off the ball quickly, reaching for the outside shoulder of linebacker. I couldn't get good leverage so I pushed him out of the way towards the sideline, washing him out. The play was only a 4-yard gain.

Two plays later, we threw an interception that Air Force converted. We were down 14-0 that quick. It definitely wasn't a good start for us.

In the second quarter, we still couldn't get into the end zone, and Air Force managed to get 10 more points on the board. The score was 24-6 at the half. We had never played so badly; I didn't know what was going on.

We managed to play a little better in the second half, but it still wasn't enough to get us out of the hole we had dug for ourselves. We tried to catch up through our run and shoot offense, but we couldn't pull it together.

Air Force won the bowl game 47-20. Our season was officially over. We had lost two out of our last three games and finished the season 10-4.

I had made a business decision, and my business at the University of Houston was over now. I had two catches for 33 yards, one touchdown, and two blocked kicks—plus a lot of growing pains and lessons learned. The season hadn't gone the way I imagined.

I still hoped I'd get a crack at the NFL. But only time was going to tell. I walked to the locker room and just sat there.

Now what?

CHAPTER 18

TRYNA' GO PRO—AGAIN

I hadn't walked out of the stadium yet when my phone started buzzing in my pocket. I looked at it and saw I already had two messages. This call was from a funky area code I never seen before. I answered the call, even though I didn't recognize the number.

"Hello?" I said, wondering who it could be.

"Hello, Fendi, my name is—"

Before I could even hear the gentleman's name, my line beeped from another incoming call.

"Hold on, sir."

"Fendi! Wassup brotha!"

"Who's this?" I asked.

"I'm an NFL agent, based out of Chicago," the second man said. "We've been tracking your progress throughout the season, and we're looking to represent you."

"Oh, wow!" I said. Remembering there was someone on the other line, I added, "Hold on real quick," and I clicked back over.

"Hello, sir?"

"Yes, I'm an agent based out of Florida. We represent over 100 players in the NFL."

I listened to the other two messages, and they were also from agents. Two minutes removed from my season and I already had calls from four different agents.

I can't lie: I was excited.

This was good. These calls were a good sign. They told me I was a step closer to my new dream. Something I had worked so hard to make a reality was actually going to become a reality.

I had believed in myself and rolled the dice. I wasn't going to stop now.

I needed to sit down with my dad and figure out the best plan before I did anything, but it was encouraging that agents were calling me.

Their interest told me I had a chance at the next level: the NFL.

I wasn't invited to any senior all-star games such as the Senior Bowl or the East-West Shrine game, but I wasn't surprised. I had hardly played.

The NFL combine was another pre-draft event, and I didn't get invited to that, either. I had thought I'd be able to make more noise coming to UH, but the cookie hadn't crumbled that way.

Even though scouts came to see me throughout the year, I never got the playing exposure I anticipated when I came to Houston but I did learn lot.

I still knew I had a shot. It was just a matter of where it was going to come from.

Pro day.

As an unknown with no post-season all-star game invite, I really had to put all my energy into my pro day. That was my Super Bowl, and I knew it. This time around, I knew what to expect.

And I had to find an agent. As a NFL draft hopeful, I had to find someone who truly believed in me.

More agents called, but after talking it over with my dad, I decided to go with a group based out of Houston. They were right up the road, and we heard great things about their representation. They had signed four other guys, so I knew I would get the attention I needed. They saw a lot of potential in me despite my lack of playing time at Houston, and they were excited to get me to the next level.

"Even though you didn't play much, Fendi, this year helped a whole lot more than you know," they told me. "Now we just have to promote what you're capable of after your pro day."

After I signed the dotted line I felt much better about my shot at the league this time around. I knew this year was going to be different—very different.

The NFL combine was a little less than a month away. I wasn't invited, but my main objective was to make sure I was in the best shape of my life come pro day. That was the goal.

That day was going to make or break my dream.

Once I signed with my agent, I was back to the pro day training all over again. But with a year of college football under my belt, I was much more confident. This second go 'round I was working with 100% intention of making it to the NFL—period.

This was what my conversations with Coach Levine, Griff, and Mr. Highsmith had been about. All the pondering, prayers, and contemplation was for this day to come to pass.

I had one shot. It was now or never. The time had come.

My agency supplied me with everything I needed to train for my pro day. I had pre-made meals delivered to me, workout shoes, cleats, workout gear, travel bags, gloves—you name it; I had it. If I needed it; they got it.

"You're a future pro. Gotta make sure you have everything you need."

I got more gear in one day from my agent than I had all year at UH!

"Our job, Fendi, is to supply you with anything and everything you need so you can solely focus on training. Welcome to the pro life."

"Wow. Thanks!" I was grateful, and I knew this support would allow me to focus more than ever. This was so different from the year before when I was working with Keith and Billy with one eye on the basketball court.

I had the option to workout with a combine trainer my agent provided, but I wanted something a little different. During my days at muscle beach, Coach Dennis had told me how he did all the pro day and combine training for guys who were coming out.

He said he had a specially designed program and assured me it got guys ready. He had been to combines in the past and studied the techniques to a T. He was highly confident he could get me right if I trained with him.

I asked others at UH, and they all vouched for him. It was apparent the man knew his stuff. I had a good relationship with Coach Dennis, and I knew he was a good coach from my experience in the Rice game. He had helped me so much with my blocking against them.

It didn't take long for me to make a decision about who would train me for my make-or-break day. I knew with the right training I was going to blow my stats from last year's pro day out of the water. Coach Dennis assured me I would.

My agent flew in a couple coaches to work with me for a week. They were specialists in route running and blocking. I wanted to make sure I got as much time with them as possible, since there were only in town for a week. I took a break from Coach Dennis so I could soak up all the knowledge from the specialists.

When I walked into training facility where we would be working at, I saw my draft class on the field doing some ladder work to warm up.

Oh shoot, I'm late.

There was an older gentleman talking to one of the quarterbacks as I was approaching the field. A short bow-legged white man with a blue hat, to be exact. I assumed he was one of the coaches.

"Hey, you the basketball player?"

I smirked. "Yes sir." I reached out to shake his hand. "Fendi Onobun, nice to meet you."

"Jerry Rhome. Well, hurry up and get dressed. You're late! Hop in line and follow what the other guys are doing."

The other receivers were about five minutes into the ladder warm up.

"Wassup, Big Dawg? Come get these ladders in," one of them called to me.

Coach Rhome had us start with a catching drill, pat-n-go. From there, we went right into routes.

"Alright, wide outs, you're going to start off with a twelve-yard comeback; tight ends, you guys got a ten-yard dig."

I was already having trouble cutting in and out of my breaks. The other receivers made it look so natural and easy. The other tight end ran his route well, too, even though he was primarily a blocker. I just tried to mimic them.

"Come out the break, hoopster!" Coach Rhome yelled.

It was a little tough for me. I was doing it, but my routes weren't nearly as crisp as the other guys.' There were a few routes I was naturally good at. The routes that gave me trouble were the ones where I had to break in or out at a 90-degree angle.

I wasn't familiar with these routes since I hardly ran them at Houston. I had blocked the majority of the time, and the routes I did run were drags and slam flats out of play action. These digs and in's were new to me.

I struggled making breaks at the top of my routes, and I was looking down at the yard lines on the field to catch my depth. It was pretty bad.

"Hey, son, be elusive. Add some wiggle to your routes! You look like a robot out there," Coach Rhome said. "You played basketball, right?"

I was thinking way too much and making it more complicated for myself. There was so much going on in my mind before I even started the route! I wasn't as good at route running as I had thought. I was just good at the routes I ran within my offense. Coach Rhome opened up the entire route tree for me here.

Come off the ball fast, ten yards out; break at eight, don't stand so high, pump your arms, get your head around, look the ball in...

All this, with no defense! All the thinking took away my athleticism. But knowing my routes weren't great, I wanted to correct the issue now. Coach Rhome had been a player in the NFL and had coached in the league, too. He had over fifty years of football experience. Everything he was telling me was right; it was just difficult for me to apply it right away.

"Look it in! Look it in!"

I dropped the ball. It was a rough first day, very rough. After our forty-five minutes on the field, I went over and worked on blocking with the O-line coach

"There you go, keep those hands up! Kick, kick, kick!"

I walked towards the drill watching one of the O-linemen working on kick slides and pass protection drills; it didn't look fun at all.

I introduced myself to the coach running the drill. "Hello, Coach. Fendi Onobun."

"Well hello there! You're going to work on a little pass pro with us?"

"Yes, sir," I confirmed. "That's why I'm here."

"Great!"

The other tight end and I hopped in line. To be honest, I wasn't too familiar with pass protection. Ninety-five percent of the time I had been run blocking at Houston. When I did pass pro, it was rare. I just thought of it as man-to-man defense. Well, that's how it was explained to me. I was clueless about hand position, foot leverage, and kick sliding.

"Fendi, you're up." I got in position and started to kick back.

"Whoa, whoa, whoa!" The O-line coach stopped me right away. "You're kicking way too far, and you don't have a base. Try to level your feet more so you have more balance. You'll get it, try again."

Going through the kick slides I was frustrated, not because of the coaching but because of how far behind I was. I had to remind myself that while I was training I was also *still* learning.

I had to be patient. This stuff was next level for me, and I needed to understand I was going to have more growing pains. It was just part of the process. The goal was to be ready come *pro* day, not *today*.

I was about to take another rep at pass protection.

"Wait, Fendi, let me help you out here." The O-line coach showed me where my feet needed to be, and told me where my hands should be positioned. He clarified that my eyes should follow the rushing defender.

Coach simplified everything, now I just had to do it. My third and fourth reps were better but still "stiff" according to Coach.

"Better than the first two. We still got some work to do, just keep watching and follow along."

I felt like I was holding the other guys back, and it was hard not to be frustrated with myself. With my sprain, I had missed out on this type of training during two-a-days in August. This was the type of training I needed.

My first few workouts with the position coaches were rough. Even after a season of football, there was a lot I had to catch up on technique-wise. It was evident I wasn't as experienced as some of the other guys who were training, but the position coaches were patient and worked with me.

Everything I learned was about efficiency and precision; no wasted movements. Every step mattered, hand positioning mattered, even my eye level on my routes mattered.

After all the skill work, I would watch film with Coach Rhome to go over different coverages and concepts. This wasn't combine training; I was in football 101.

As the week progressed, I was improving. I worked really hard with the coaches, and Coach Rhome started spending more time with me. To help with my cuts, he took me to a basketball court for a day.

"Alright, Fendi, let me see you hoop!"

"What?" I didn't know what he was up to.

"You're a basketball player, right? Make some cuts. Imagine that I'm passing you the ball off your cut."

It was weird. I was kind of confused at first. Coach Rhome had me make a few cuts off the baseline, then some from the elbow and the wing.

After a while, it was kind of fun. It had been a while since I stepped foot on a basketball court.

Coach Rhome wanted to see if I was as stiff on the court as I was running my routes on the field. Once he realized I wasn't, he started to put things into basketball terms when we were on the football field. I wasn't stiff and robot-like at all on the court. Basketball was something I had done my whole life, so it came naturally.

Coach even started throwing the football to me on the court. He explained to me that my cuts on the basketball court were same type of cuts on the football field: the same body movements, change of direction, and staying low. It was amazing how he broke it down for me to understand.

It was like he flipped on a light switch in my head.

Coach Rhome's patience was similar to Coach Levine's, and he really made things easy for me to comprehend. The week I spent with the coaches was so valuable; I was glad I took the time off from UH to do it.

"Fendi, I'm really excited about you," he told me. You got some natural ability, and I want to see you do well. I'm not gonna lie: when I first saw you, I thought to myself: he looks the part, but I'm not sure how much he's gonna pick up. Especially after I heard your story. But I watched you improve each and every day, and you have work ethic. I was amazed at how you progressed so quickly. I'm really excited for you."

Coming from someone with more than fifty years of experience in the game, that was pretty high praise.

The O-line coach told me to keep working. I wasn't there yet. Haha.

"I figure you'll be doing minimal blocking in the NFL. You'll probably be one of those receiving tight ends. But at least you have a good foundation of pass protection and run blocking." And he added, "You're smart. Plus, I see you want to learn, and that's encouraging."

He advised me to keep working on the things he had shown me and said I'd be asked to do it in private workouts. I did understand the basics of blocking, and I learned how to kick slide from both sides, but I was definitely going to have to work at it.

I wasn't sure what was going to be asked of me in the NFL, but I knew I needed to be able to do it all. Blocking was a big part of the tight end position. The time spent with these coaches had definitely been worth it.

Coach Rhome said he would come back the week before the combine and check on me. "Next time I see you, you better be breakin' out of those in and out routes like you're on the basketball court!"

Pre-Draft post workout picture (left to right) Brody Eldridge, My Dad, Coach Jerry Rhome, Me, Duke Calhoun, Kerry Meier, Jevan Sneed. February 2010. Houston, Texas

"Ha ha, I got you, Coach."

"I'm serious," he said. "You get better! Don't fall back!"

"I won't!" I promised.

Once the coaches left, I was back at UH working with Coach Dennis.

"Wait till you guys see the numbers you pull in these drills when I'm done with you," he told us. "You're not going to believe it."

None of us were going to the NFL combine, so we had nearly two months to train. Coach Jackson didn't have an exact pro day date yet, but he knew it would be sometime in March.

Coach Dennis pre-tested us in every pro day event to get baseline numbers on us. I ran a 4.54 in the 40-yard dash, which was pretty fast. My vertical jump was 34 inches. I benched 225 lbs. 11 times, and broad jumped 10 feet 2 inches. My short shuttle was 4.41 and my 3-cone drill was 7.01.

Some areas I was naturally good at, and others I needed work in. Nonetheless, Dennis guaranteed I was going to improve my numbers in every single event if I worked as hard as he expected me to.

We started off pretty slow but picked it up as the weeks went on. I was so determined. I had never been so focused in my life. All I could keep thinking about was pro day in March. This was going to be my one shot to make it happen, and I was giving it everything I had.

Each week Coach Dennis was tweaking my technique and making adjustments on my form for the drills. We worked at it day in and day out. I still needed to improve, but by week seven I was a lot better than what I was at week three.

I was getting so much drill work but my skill and position work wasn't getting nearly as much attention. I was by myself and it was hard to work on those things alone. I tried to work on the things the O-line coach taught me but it was hard to see if I was actually kick sliding the right way.

The tips Coach Rhome left me with were great but I didn't know if I was cutting as low as he would have liked. One of the graduate assistants at UH would help me from time to time, but it just wasn't the same

I was training in the weight room with Coach Dennis when Coach Levine stopped by.

"Hey Fendi, come up to my office when you get a chance, I want to talk to you about something."

"Alright Coach."

I wondered what it was.

Maybe more good news from scouts?

I didn't know. Most scouts at this time were getting ready for the combine, so I had no clue. I finished my workout and went up to Levine's office.

Knock, knock, knock...

"What's up Coach?"

"You've gotten bigger what are you weighing?" he asked.

"About 250. I'm training hard, Coach. Pro day is next month."

"I know. Well you look great. How are the workouts?"

"They're going really well," I told him. "Coach Dennis is doing a great job."

"I knew he'd be good for you. But what about your tight end stuff? You have anybody working with you on that?" he asked.

"Um, no. Not at the moment. I worked out with some coaches a few weeks back, but I don't know of anyone who could help me right now, so I just try to do what I can by myself."

"I figured, and that's why I called you up. I met a gentleman at a coaching clinic this past weekend by the name of David Sloan. He's a former NFL tight end who lives here in Houston and is just getting into coaching. I told him about you and asked if he had the time, could he work with you."

"Wow, really coach?" I lit up when I heard the news. "Man, that would be awesome if he could!"

"I know!" Levine said. "That's exactly what you need, someone with actual experience who could help you hone your skills and build on what you've already learned. Now, he's married with children, so I don't know how much time he'll have, but here."

Levine gave me the number.

"Give him a call and see what he says. He told me he'd love to meet with you and talk about it."

"Coach Levine, thanks! I appreciate it! A lot!"

"Sure thing, let me know what he says, will ya."

"Alright!" I promised him.

Wow.

God is so good. I had just been thinking to myself how much I needed something like this! Working with the coaches a few weeks back had been good, but they were only here for a week.

I needed something more hands-on and this couldn't have been a better opportunity. As soon as I got home I Googled David Sloan to see who he was before I actually met with him.

This dude was a legit pro. He played nine seasons in the NFL and was a pro bowl tight end.

This was perfect!

I gave him a ring, but he didn't answer, so I left a voicemail. He got back to me within a couple days and told me he'd love to help me out. I couldn't wait to meet him.

That Sunday we met at the UH practice field. I didn't know what to expect. I just wanted to soak everything in, because I knew his information would be valuable. We warmed up for a bit before we got started.

"Alright, Fendi, let's see your stance."

I set up, and he said, "Everything should be based off the inside of your foot when it comes to your stance, coming in and out of routes, and blocking. These are your insteps. They're the most valuable part of your footwork."

Coach Sloan showed me how to plant off my insteps in my routes, and they instantly improved. My footwork was better, and I had more power in my blocking. It was the first time I had ever heard of the term but it was so helpful.

Aside from all the combine stuff I was doing with Coach Dennis, Coach Sloan was showing me how to become a better tight end. This was what I needed.

"All these things I'm showing you might not help you on your pro day, but they're going to help during your workouts."

Every Sunday we met and worked on different things. Sloan showed me so much. We worked on pass-blocking drills, run-blocking drills, and we simulated different releases off of the line. It was amazing. In just the few sessions I had with him I learned so much more about the tight end position. He taught me the tricks of the trade.

I knew all the stuff he was showing me was going to help me in the future.

"Fendi I like your work ethic," he told me. "You're very raw, but keep working at it. As far as getting drafted, that may be a long shot. I don't know. But don't worry about that. Focus on trying to make a team's roster. It doesn't matter how you get there."

Deep down inside, I still felt I could get drafted. I believed I had a shot, even after only one season of football.

But Coach Sloan was right, being drafted wasn't the only way into the NFL. It was just a personal goal of mine. I didn't share it with anyone else, but I wanted to do the unthinkable.

I wanted to get drafted into the NFL.

Working out with David Sloan gave me a complete workout regimen, and with my pro day around the corner, I couldn't have been on a better plan. The NFL scouting combine was the following weekend.

I wasn't invited, but it was probably for the better. I had that much more time to prepare for pro day.

After watching the combine and seeing the competition, the intensity of my workouts rose. I got a chance to work out with Coach Sloan a few more times, and I got more familiar with the little nuances of the position.

Working with a pro-bowl tight end, I learned so much. His teaching was a Godsend. The skill work with him was paying off, and I was getting better and better.

Coach Dennis re-tested us after we had been training with him for nine weeks. I was definitely expecting to see some improvement. We did all our tests on grass just like when we first tested.

All my numbers improved, but they weren't where I wanted them to be.

"Trust me Fendi, we're doing the test on grass for a reason. When you test on the turf your numbers will improve immensely," Coach Dennis said.

My 40-yard dash time went from 4.54 to 4.49; that would have been 2nd place for tight ends at the combine. My bench press improved from 11 reps to 15. I also improved in my 3 cone and short shuttle times as well.

I still hadn't hit my goal numbers, but my times had gone down. I continued with the workout regimen and kept my tunnel vision. I was soaking in everything I could from Coach Dennis and Coach Sloan. I stayed persistent.

Coach Sloan was even impressed with the vast improvement I made from just five workouts with him.

"Fendi, I'm really amazed at how natural you look now. You're doing a great job out there. Each workout you're improving, and that's a good sign."

That following Monday, Coach Jackson came out to the field while we were working out and said, "Hey fellas, I got a date for the pro day! We're going to have it on March 30th! Get ready!"

I finally had a specific date to look forward to. Nothing else mattered to me but March 30, 2010. The day couldn't come soon enough.

I was going to shock everyone.

CHAPTER **19**
PRO DAY 2.0

Pro day was less than two weeks away. I wanted to focus on getting stronger and faster, while perfecting all of the drills I was going to be tested on. Coach Rhome stayed in contact with me throughout training to make sure I was working on the things he showed me. Thanks to the help of Coach Sloan, that part was coming together.

"Fendi, I told you I would be here for you. I'm booking my ticket right now so I can be at your pro day. And I'm not only coming to watch your pro day; I'm coming to *run it.* I know exactly what those scouts want to see you do and I'm going to make sure they see it all!

"You are too talented and too fast to not have these scouts see you do it all! Not only are we going to have you run routes from the tight end position, I'm going to have you run routes from the slot, out wide, and we're going to have you working in motion. I've seen you do it, now its time for them to!"

Coach Rhome was adamant about exposing my ability. He knew I hadn't gotten to show much at UH, and he wanted to make sure we did everything possible to make up for it.

I spent the last week cleaning up a few things with Coach Dennis. Rhome made sure my routes were right, and Coach Sloan gave me a few more pointers before the big day.

I felt really good about all my drills. I did a little bit of lifting to maintain my strength, but the work had been done. It had been a long challenging ten weeks. I had disciplined myself physically and mentally for the reward of one day.

Now that one day was only two days away. It all came down to this. I was ready to showcase myself in front of NFL scouts again, and this time I was fully prepared.

I had been here before, but this situation was different. I had a chip on my shoulder.

This pro day was driven by something deeper. This was personal. I wanted to do the unthinkable.

All the emotions and frustrations I endured from the day I decided to give football a try were packed like dynamite into this one day. This day was the reason I walked onto University of Houston's football team. This was why I had pushed myself to learn the game of football. This was the business I came here for; for this one day; a shot at the NFL.

March 30, 2010; Pro day.

I woke up at 6 a.m., ready to go. I fell to my knees thanking God for the opportunity. He had truly brought me full circle. I made myself some breakfast and drove to UH to get ready for pro day.

The time had finally come. I was so focused and ready that there was absolutely nothing that was going to break my concentration.

I had been waiting for this moment for a long time. I didn't care about stats, all-star games, or post-season accolades. All I had was this one day, and as God was my witness, I was going make the most of it.

I went into the training room to get warmed up and stretched out. I saw all the scouts trickling in. The Saints, Colts, and the Panthers all walked into the building at the same time. Right behind them was a herd of scouts, the Falcons, Bengals, Dolphins, Browns, Chiefs and Texans... there were so many!

Although I was screaming with excitement inside, I kept my focus. I had a show to put on.

There were eleven participants for the annual pro day and about twenty scouts present to evaluate. A couple of them spoke to me beforehand and asked me a few questions. I figured they were trying to see where my head was. If anything, they knew I was serious about this pro day and I meant business.

Similar to last year's pro day at Arizona, the scouts started off by taking our measurements. I came in at 6 feet 5.25 inches and 252 pounds. I was about five pounds heavier than last year plus a season of football this time around.

Up next was the standing vertical jump. My personal goal was 38 inches. I jumped and got 37.5.

I walked over to the next station; the broad jump. I knew I would kill it; it was my strongest event. My first jump was a 10'9". It was a tight end record at the combine, but I wanted to break 11". I had one more chance to do it.

"Wow!" A scout said as I landed. "11 feet and 1 inch!"

I knew no other tight end in the country had broad jumped that far, and it was personal record for me. Feeling pretty good about myself, I walked over to the next event: the bench press.

The previous week I hit 16 reps, and my goal today was 18; I was hoping my adrenaline would carry me to 19 or 20. There were a few guys ahead of me, and my anticipation grew.

"Onobun, you're next!" The scout called my name. *Finally, my turn.*

Everyone was cheering me on. The first 10 reps of 225 were relatively easy. I hit my second wind at the eleventh rep. I knew I had to push through; I began to slow down at 14. I tried to push out a few more. I stopped at 16. I couldn't physically push any more.

"Agh-h-h-h-h! *Shoot!*"

Coach Dennis racked the weight for me. A bit frustrated, I went on to the next drill. I had to keep pushing.

We migrated to the turf for all the agility drills. I noticed there was a much bigger crowd when we got out there. This was really becoming a show.

The first field drill was the 40-yard dash, the most hyped drill of them all. I didn't know what I was going to run, but I needed to push out of my start, run as fast as I possibly could, and keep my form on point.

Coach Dennis had told me that if I was relaxed I would run just fine. I felt good about this one. I was focused, and definitely relaxed. I was the sixth man to go out of the eleven.

It was time. I felt light and explosive. I was going to rip this turf into shreds. Already warm and stretched out, I was ready to go. I took my mark and waited for the OK to go.

I said a quick prayer, then waited: three seconds, two seconds, gone! My start felt great! I dug my feet into the ground to gain speed. I kept my form and reached top speed at the 25-30 yard mark.

All eyes were on me. I finished through the 40-yard line like a track star. It felt good, but instantly I felt I could have run faster. Something didn't feel right.

As I walked back to the starting point, I looked to see if anyone had my time.

"4.5!" I overheard.

Coach Rhome came running to me. "I clocked you at 4.5, Fendi. The scouts are going crazy."

That was a good time, but I knew I could run faster. Something hadn't felt right, and I knew exactly what it was: I didn't punch my legs through like Coach Dennis taught me.

It was new, so I had to remind myself to do it. That would have generated more power and given me a better time. I was going to make sure I did it on my second turn. There was no doubt that I was going to run in the 4.4s.

"Fendi Onobun, you're up again!"

I had done all my drills in two pairs of tights. Before I approached the start line, I took off my gray tights, revealing the black ones underneath. It felt like a transformation; I was in a new mode. My whole mentality had just changed in that moment. I was going to run a 4.4.

Before I took the line I said another quick prayer, waited three seconds, and took off!

This time I was punching my knees as hard as I could while keeping my form intact. It felt so fluent. When I hit that 40th yard line, it just felt faster—*way faster.*

I heard someone in the crowd whisper "4.45" as I was walking back.

Coach Rhome came to me. "Holy Smokes, kid! I clocked you at 4.44!"

I smiled in satisfaction. I wasn't sure what the scouts clocked me at, but I knew it was under 4.5. After that second 40, I think I had the attention of every scout in the field house. All of them were surprised to see a guy my size run that fast.

Eleven scouts followed me to my next drill, the 20-yard shuttle.

The average time for tight ends in this drill was around 4.25 to 4.30 seconds. When I finished the drill, I clocked in at 4.17 seconds.

"That kid was movin'!" I heard the buzz around me.

I didn't want to celebrate. I had to get to the next station, which was the three-cone drill.

I didn't set goal times for these two agility drills; I just wanted to move as fast as I could and let the time take care of itself.

Most of the tight ends at the combine did this drill around the 6.9 second mark. I clocked in at a 6.78. Things were looking good for me, and I was doing exactly what I intended to do.

But I still had more work to do. My pro day wasn't over yet.

A scout from the Chiefs pulled me to the side and had me do some tight end blocking drills. A slew of scouts came over to watch me. It was like none of them were interested in watching anyone else. This day was all business, and that was the mindset I had.

Coach Sloan told me they would do this.

The Chiefs scout wanted me to go through some blocking techniques. The blocking drills were very similar to the things I had worked on before with Coach Levine and David Sloan. I was simulating blocks as hard as I possibly could; driving the bag and the Chiefs' scout at least eight yards down the field every time.

One of my blocks even lifted the scout off the ground. After all the repetitions, the scout seemed satisfied—and exhausted from trying to hold my blocks.

"Good job, son, I just wanted to see you block a little bit."

"Thank you, sir," I responded.

During the season I had blocked the majority of the time, so I felt comfortable doing the drill. What I was looking forward to the most at this pro day was showing these scouts I could catch. I hadn't gotten to do too much of that at UH, so no one knew what I could do.

That was about to change.

All the drill work was done, and it was time to run routes. I knew everything would be on point. Coach Rhome had scripted ten different routes for me to run from the tight end position, the slot, and out wide.

We started off in a huddle and broke out to our spots. I couldn't wait to run my first route. I had a flat route right to the sideline.

The ball hit my hands, then bounced off them and fell to the turf.

"Ah-h-h-h-h-h-h-h!" I screamed as the ball slipped through my fingertips.

C'mon, Fen!

I was excited. That's all it was. I had to reel it in a bit and control the jitters.

I picked the ball up and ran back to huddle for the next route. I caught my second and third passes and was able to get into a groove with the quarterback. After that, we connected on every ball thrown my direction. I even caught a 40-yard go route; a throw I had been struggling to catch all week.

Pro day 2.0 ended well. I was satisfied with the work I had left on the field.

The rest was up to the Man above.

Nine teams wanted to sit down and meet with me afterwards; it was a long, long day.

By the time I was done, I was the only player in the facility; everyone else had left. I was hoping that with the type of attention I was receiving, something good was going to come of it.

I didn't know which team liked me the most or seemed the most interested, but I knew someone would give me a shot.

That night I got a phone call from Mr. Highsmith the Green Bay scout,

"Fendi, am I hearing this correctly?" he asked. "You ran a 4.44 and 4.48 forty?"

I laughed. "Yes sir, I sure did!"

"Wow, son! I heard you were fast, but I didn't know you were that fast. Good job! Everybody is talking about the numbers you put up today. Now you just gotta play the waiting game and see where you end up. But with numbers like that, you'll go somewhere, trust me."

It was good to hear that from him.

My agent told me, "Fendi, your numbers are off the charts!" Fourteen teams approached him inquiring about me.

A few days later, my 40-yard dash time and pro day results caught like wildfire. My phone was blowing up from different scouts in the NFL.

Now they knew who I was.

Onobun shines in football pro day workout

Performance on gridiron earns UA hoops player NFL team visit

By Lance Madden
Arizona Daily Wildcat

The transition from the hardwood to the gridiron is starting to pick up some speed for Fendi Onobun.

After weeks of personal anticipation, the former Arizona basketball player finally got his chance to show NFL scouts his abilities, despite a shortage of playing time during one season as tight end at the University of Houston

He certainly didn't hold back.

Onobun's performance in the Yeoman Field House in the Athletics/Alumni Center in Houston, Texas during the Cougars' official pro day workout on Tuesday earned him an April 8 visit with the Seattle Seahawks and a visit with the New York Giants on April 11.

More than a dozen NFL teams were represented while Onobun and 10 of his Houston teammates worked out.

"It was stressful," Onobun told the Daily Wildcat. "It's just an intense

atmosphere. You want to do so well. This is what you've been training for. You make sure you're eating right and lifting right.

"All those scouts are watching your every move," he continued. "You want to perform the best you can, but at the same time you want to have fun and be loose.

But you want to realize you don't get many opportunities to do this."

After just four hours of sleep, Onobun was still able to run a faster 40-yard dash (4.48 seconds) than all tight end invitees at the NFL Combine save for Pittsburgh's Dorin Dickerson. He would have placed fourth among tight ends at the Combine in the vertical jump, second in the 3-cone

ONOBUN'S PRO DAY STATS
Body 6-foot-6, 252 pounds
40-yard dash 4.48 seconds
225-pound bench 16 repetitions
20-yard shuttle 4.15 seconds
60-yard shuttle 11.64 seconds
3-cone drill 6.78 seconds
Broad jump 11 feet, 1 inch
Vertical jump 37.5 inches

drill, second in the 60-yard shuttle, first in the 20-yard shuttle and first in the broad jump.

Onobun ran 14 routes during the workout and caught all but the first pass from quarterback Blake Joseph from Sam Houston State. He said he had a few scouts pull him to the side to talk to him after his workout.

"I was nervous. I was jittery, but that was normal," Onobun said. "Once we got into the drills my confidence grooved and I got more confidence. After I got through all that I was just doing me."

Onobun, who is being projected as a late NFL Draft pick or a free agent signee, had his mother, father and two little brothers on hand to watch his workout, along with several friends. Cowboys tight end Martellus Bennett,

who went to school with Onobun, also took in the pro day event with his father.

Current Houston Rocket forward Jordan Hill, who played for the UA basketball team from 2006-09, couldn't make it because he had a team shootaround.

Onobun had a chance to play basketball professionally overseas, but decided to take advantage of his size and athletic ability. After four years at the UA, he was granted a transfer to Houston, where he played for the football team for a full season, taking in two catches for 33 yards and a touchdown, not to mention a wealth of experience.

"I've learned so much in the last eight months," he said. "I look at my form in my first day of two-a-days and I didn't have any form. I look at myself today on film and I've come a long way. I've been blessed. God has given me a real opportunity."

But Onobun knows he has far to go.

"Now that my pro day is over, it doesn't mean I've crossed the finish line," he said. "I'm just beginning."

Pro Day workout article written by Lance Madden.
(*Arizona Daily Wildcat*) 2010.

CHAPTER **20**

CLOSER TO
MY DREAM

There couldn't have been a better time than this to go from an unknown to a sleeper in the draft.

A lot of scouts didn't know much about me. I hadn't played much at UH, and I only had one season of collegiate football under my belt. The draft was less than three weeks away and teams had to do their homework on me.

My agent told me a few teams wanted to fly me in for pre draft visits, while a few others wanted to come to Houston and work me out. I was all for it.

Within a matter of days, everything had changed. I was just so thankful. I had some ups and downs during the season, along with the frustrations of not playing much. But God is just, and *this* was exactly what I had come to UH for.

This was why I made my "business decision," and *this* was why I passed up overseas basketball. I truly believed I was getting closer to my dream.

I was in the film room studying film and sharpening my understanding of the game.

My agent stressed to me how important it was for me to have FBI, Football Intelligence.

Knock. Knock. Knock.

"Who is it?" I called, but I didn't hear anyone say anything.

Knock. Knock. Knock.

I ignored the knocking on the door. Whenever Dee would go to work and leave me home alone, she told me to stay inside and not open the door for anyone.

Some days the nanny didn't show up, and on those days I kept the doors locked. I'd eat ramen noodles and watch TV until Dee got home.

Knock. Knock. Knock.

"Poops open up. It's me."

Since I heard Dee's voice, I got up and looked through the peephole. She was there, and there were two guys in black suits white shirts and black ties standing with her.

"It's okay. Open the door."

I was scared. I opened the door. The three of them entered the apartment.

"What's going on, Dee?" I asked.

"Everything is OK, Fendi," she answered, but clearly something was up.

The gentlemen asked me to put my shoes on and come with them.

"Poops, follow the man. It's okay."

I didn't know if I was in trouble, or if my mom was in trouble. But I knew this wasn't good.

"What about Dee? What's going on? Where am I going?!"

I followed the gentlemen. Their cars were police cars. They put me in one, and Dee went into the other.

We were in trouble.

The guy asked me a few questions about where we had lived in Vegas, how long we had been there, and what I had done. I was worried because I thought they knew about the mischief I caused at the apartment complex.

"Am I going to jail, sir?"

"No, buddy," the gentleman said. "We're going to take you to protective services for a little bit. You'll be somewhere safe, with other kids and a school."

I was in a police car, away from both of my parents now; I was scared.

I didn't know what was going on, but the gentleman took me to get some ice cream before we went to the protective services place. Whenever I saw a cop car it usually wasn't a good sign, so when I had seen two of them sitting outside, I definitely thought I was in trouble.

But the gentleman just kept telling me they wanted me located at a safe place.

———————————

"Fendi, you in there?"

I walked up to the UH film room door and opened it.

"Fendi! Remember me?"

I looked at him trying to remember where I had seen this familiar face.

Then it hit me.

This was the first scout I ever spoke to. He was the guy from the New York Jets who had taken my measurements at pro day last year in Tucson. I couldn't believe I was seeing him again. He had come to congratulate me on such a great workout. He told me word was getting around fast about me.

"Fendi, I didn't think you'd come around. I'm being honest. I thought you had a ways to go, and I thought at best you'd come in as an undrafted guy.

"But I saw you grow and get more comfortable. And after your pro day, I was stunned by your results. It's amazing what you've come here and done since you left Arizona."

"Thank you, sir! Thank you," I replied.

"I guess you were a hidden gem. And after a workout like that, there's no doubt in my mind that you'll get drafted! Don't be surprised if you get a call from us on draft day." He smiled. "I'd like to extend a pre-draft visit invitation for you to come to New York. How does that sound?"

I just stared at him for a second. I was speechless.

"Well...?" he asked.

I snapped out of it. "Oh, yes! Absolutely! I'd love to come!"

"Great! We'll see you in New York! Someone will be calling you from our offices soon."

WOW.

I knew it was nothing but God. Nothing but. Everything that was happening gave me more confirmation that I had ultimately made the right decision.

The Jets were the first team to extend a pre draft visit. Later that week my agent told me the Seahawks wanted me to come in and see them as well.

"Great, when's the visit?"

"Tomorrow."

"Oh, wow! Okay."

"A representative from the club should be calling you in the next few minutes to schedule your traveling plans."

It was like being recruited all over again. As fun as it was, I knew it was business. Every move I made was being watched.

The next morning, I was on a plane to Seattle, Washington, to meet with the Seahawks. I met with Coach Pete Carroll, followed by a meeting with the tight ends coach. We watched film on how they used their tight ends and learned a few of their concepts.

I wasn't sure how interested he was in me, but I could tell he didn't know much of my story. After the meet-and-greet, I headed to lunch at the cafeteria.

"Hey Fendi, how's it going? I believe we spoke about a year ago. I think you were trying to come in for a try-out or something of that sort?"

I knew exactly what he was talking about.

"O-o-o-o-o yeah! I remember quite well!" I smirked. "You're the guy who told me last year I'd be better off pursuing basketball."

"Yeah, I am," he said. "Well, I take that back. You made me eat my words! We get a lot of athletes like that, and none of them ever make it through. I obvious-ly see you're a special case. Welcome to Seattle."

I knew he was surprised I was there. I remembered what he had told me, and it was ironic how it had all come full circle; but this time I was a draft prospect! What were the odds?

God... you are too good!

Coach Carroll appeared to be a very energetic coach. I wasn't sure how their tight ends coach felt about me, but that didn't matter at this point. I knew they were interested. And for my first NFL visit, it was a great trip.

When I got back home, it was back to my regular scheduled program with Coach Dennis. I didn't have to worry about combine drills anymore, since my pro day was done. Coach Dennis was helping me stay in shape.

I had a few days to workout then I going to visit with the Jets. Two days before I left for New York my agent called.

"Get ready for two more trips, Big Man. Add the Giants and the Panthers to the list."

"When?"

"Well, since you're going to New York, we'll knock out two birds with one stone. You'll visit the Jets and the Giants on the same trip. We're still working on a date for Carolina. The Giants will be first, then you'll go see the Jets afterwards."

This was crazy!

All the attention was unbelievable! Not only was I going to see the Jets, but I was seeing the Giants and the Panthers too! I had no words for what was going on, but things were looking really good. Getting draft-ed really felt like a possibility.

The next morning, I was in the Big Apple with fifteen other prospects visiting with the Giants.

Once we got to the hotel there was a scheduled dinner for players to meet the head coach and the rest of the coaching staff. The Giants are such a storied franchise; it was an honor to be one of the fifteen invited for a pre draft visit.

During the dinner, a tall gentleman approached me. "Fendi, how's it going? I'm the tight ends coach here."

"Hey, Coach. Pleasure to meet you."

He spoke with me briefly and told me his experience in the NFL. He had been coaching the position for a long time in the NFL, and it was clear that he was very knowledgeable about the position. He was known as one of the best in the business.

"I'll be seeing you tomorrow in the tight ends room around 11:00, correct?"

"Yes, sir." I replied.

In Seattle the tight ends coach had showed us some film on how they used their tight ends in their offense. The meeting was about twenty minutes tops. I figured the Giants would do the same thing, but I wasn't sure; every team is different.

The next morning after my physical and breakfast, my 11 o'clock meeting was ten minutes away. I began to head towards the tight ends room.

OK, now where's the tight ends room?

The facility was like a miniature maze. Walking around looking for the room I saw other position meeting rooms.

Quarterbacks...

Wide Receivers...

Running Backs... No.

Ok, here we go. Tight Ends! Found it.

I walked in to what looked like a classroom. There were five desks, a table, and a big white board. Behind the five desks sat the coach's desk. He had already written some things on the board: a bunch of half shaded O's with some letters representing a defense.

I didn't know if it was for us or not, but I was the first one in the room, so I patiently waited for him to walk in.

Seconds later, another prospect walked in, followed by the tight ends coach.

"Good morning, gentlemen," said the coach. "Here, the tight ends are tough, disciplined, and fundamental. I don't know how they do it anywhere else, but I can assure you that here we play the game of football, and we play it the fundamental way. We block, we're smart, and we make our team better doing it."

My eyes didn't blink for almost fifteen seconds. It felt like I was listening to a drill sergeant. We watched a little film, but not much. We spent the majority of our time on the white board; something I struggled with.

"Fendi, draw a defensive over front for me on the white board."

He then asked me to draw an under front. I hardly knew where to draw the defensive linemen. It exposed me.

He was using terms like "inside shade," "3 technique," "nickel," and "dime." I had nothing to draw for him.

I could see his frustration, but I told him I had never heard of some of the terms he was using. It was embarrassing, but I was being honest.

At Houston, I had been told five plays to memorize: three route concepts and two zone blocking schemes. I didn't even think about any fronts. And the only techniques I was familiar with were the ones in front of the tight end.

I knew I was going to be tested, but I wasn't ready. My meeting with the Giants was one of the toughest meetings I've ever had. I was happy when it was over.

I wasn't confident I'd be hearing from them anytime soon, but my visit really put the situation into perspective for me.

I'm going to have to play catch up with the X's and O's fast!

My next stop was with the New York Jets. This was my third team visit. I had to do another routine physical with the team doctor and meet with the training staff afterwards.

I walked into the training room and saw Ladanian Tomlison doing rehab. It totally caught me off guard; I always saw him scoring touchdowns on TV and now I was in the same room with him; I couldn't believe it.

Once I finished all the medical stuff, I met with some coaches. The first coach I had a meeting with was the special teams coach. After that meeting, I was escorted to the tight ends coach.

"You must be Fendi! Welcome to New York."

We spoke briefly about my sports history and my novelty in the game of football; he knew my background for the most part and didn't waste any time getting to business.

"Here, take this pen and notebook."

He began to teach me their offense right off the bat.

"You're going to be quizzed on this later, so make sure you gather as much information as possible. I know it's a lot, but do the best you can."

"Yes, sir."

Whoa.

Startled a bit, I began writing all the things Coach was explaining to me. He started off with all of their two tight-end formations. At UH we only had two tight end sets, "Deuce" and "Slot." The Jets had seven.

The "H," or the pass-catching tight end, determined the name of the formation. I actually understood it pretty well. Overall it wasn't too bad, once I understood the concepts. He taught me a few play calls. I had learned so much in twenty-five minutes.

After my meeting, the assistant offensive coordinator quizzed me on the information I just learned. It went pretty well, and I was pleased.

Once that meeting finished, I had a sit down with Coach Rex Ryan in his office. I wasn't expecting him to be as laid back as he was. Word was that he was a players' coach, and I could see how he had gotten this reputation.

We had a good conversation. He told me if I didn't remember anything else to remember this: "As long as you're willing to play hard, you can play for me. You're obviously talented, or you wouldn't be in my office right now. If you can do that, you can be a Jet."

I got back home and worked out with Coach Dennis for one day before I had to fly out to North Carolina. I figured more than likely this visit would be my last, since the draft was less than a week away plus all this traveling was exhausting me.

The Panthers were the team Coach Levine had been with before he came to UH, and he was good friends with their tight ends coach. I got to Charlotte on a Sunday afternoon. It was quiet and country-like. I liked it.

I knew that Carolina wasn't known for their tight end play, but maybe they were looking to make a change. I was by myself on this trip, the only draft prospect visiting.

My first meeting was early with the tight ends coach. We didn't get on the white board or watch film right away. He gave me a tour of the facility, and we talked as we walked. After the tour he introduced me briefly to all of the offensive coaches.

The visit started to feel reminiscent of a college-recruiting trip: super relaxed. We watched some film on their tight ends from the previous season. Eight out of ten times, they were blocking.

Coach told me they were looking to open up their offense a bit with another receiving threat. "Six times out of ten we're running the ball, and the other four times it's going to our number one receiver, Steve Smith."

We went back upstairs where the other offensive coaches were, and I had a one-on-one with the offensive coordinator.

"I'm not going to lie to you. I don't know who you are, and I've never heard of you before. How long have you been playing football?"

"One year, sir."

"What do you bring to the table at the tight end position?" He started shooting question after question to me.

"What special teams you play?"

"How can you help our team win?"

"So you didn't start playing football until last year at twenty-three years of age? This was your first year playing?"

There were so many questions.

———————

"Fendi… you okay?"

"What's your date of birth?"

"Can you remember all the places you and your mother have lived while in Vegas?"

I was afraid. It felt like I was in trouble. I was sitting in a chair next to this office lady. She kept asking me more and more questions. Every response was being entered into a computer. My palms were getting sweaty, and I was nervous. I didn't know if I was going to see my mom or my dad ever again.

"This place is very safe for you my, dear. Here at CPS, we will take good care of you."

"Am I staying here?"

"For the time being, darling," the office lady responded.

All I could think about were my parents. Now that I was away from Dee I didn't know what was going to happen. The phone rang, and the lady picked up.

"Hey, we're just about done. I'll be bringing him shortly." Then she hung up.

What's going on?!

I saw other kids outside the window of the room where I was sitting. My feet dangled from the chair. I just wanted the questions to stop.

"How old are you, Fendi?"

"I'm seven."

"Can you remember the last time you saw your father?"

"Around my birthday, in November."

I got a small taste of the brash honesty that comes with the NFL.

The Carolina coordinator told me my lack of experience wouldn't make their ball club. I knew I was athletic enough to play in the league; I just needed a chance. It looked like it that wouldn't be happening in North Carolina.

I met the head coach for about five minutes or so over lunch. I knew I wouldn't be hearing from them anytime soon. It was definitely my weirdest trip thus far.

I was back home in Houston with the draft only days away. This moment couldn't come soon enough! As soon as I landed from Charlotte I reached for my phone to text Coach Dennis about the next day's workout time.

Before I could finish sending the message, I received a text from my agent that read: "The Rams and the Texans want to work you out tomorrow at 11:30 at the UH field house."

What?

"ARE YOU SERIOUS RIGHT NOW?" I responded.

His reply was, "Yup."

The news was good, but I had mixed feelings about it. I really didn't want to work out for teams this late in the process; the draft was only two days away!

I was exhausted. In the last two weeks, I had just traveled all over the country visiting teams. I thought I was done. I wanted to relax, but then I remembered what

I was doing two days before the draft the year before: scrambling to get my You Tube workout to scouts, hoping for a call.

Now I had scouts scrambling to work me out. With the draft only 48 hours away, I was blessed to be in this position opposed to the one I was in the year before.

With the draft being this close, these two teams *had* to be highly interested in me.

Texans?

Rams?

Hmmmmm?

Maybe my childhood dream of playing for my hometown team would be fulfilled after all! But it would be a football team, not the Rockets!

I got a good night's rest so I could be fresh for the workout the next morning.

April 20, 2010

11:15 a.m. came quick. I was jogging across the field, warming up with Coach Dennis. I saw my agent walk into the field house with a few guys behind him. They were the scouts from both teams. My adrenaline shot up when I saw them. I was instantly ready.

It was time to for my job interview with the St. Louis Rams and the Houston Texans.

"Are you ready to go, Fendi? You all warmed up?" the Rams coach asked me.

"Yes, sir!"

"Good! He extended his hand towards me, I'm Frank Leonard; the tight ends coach for the St. Louis Rams."

"Nice to meet you sir."

"Lets get to work!"

Both representatives had me start off with a few bag drills, which was standard in most tight end workouts.

"Every time I yell HIT, I want you punch the bag from your knees as aggressively and as violently as you possibly can."

HIT!... HIT!... HIT!... HIT!... HIT!

"Good, Fendi! Good explosion!"

Next, both teams simulated another blocking drill with dummy defensive bags. The workout was going well, and it was beginning to draw a crowd.

The Rams coach was so high-energy that he took over the workout. The Texans scout slowly became a spectator as the Rams representative put me through the rest of the workout.

Deeper into the workout the crowd at the field house got even bigger. It was like my pro day all over again. I didn't let it distract my focus, though; I was in the middle of a job interview.

After all the blocking drills, the Rams coach had me run a few routes and catch footballs in place. The forty-five-minute workout was taxing, but I did well and didn't drop one ball.

The representatives from the Rams seemed pleased. I didn't get much feedback from the Texans but I gave my all, hoping I left a good impression with both teams. I shook both coaches' hands and thanked them for the opportunity.

"Hey, Fendi, is there a room or an office where we can go talk?" Coach Leonard asked. "I want to ask you a few questions."

I took him upstairs to the football offices where we sat and spoke for a bit. He asked me about my football experience at UH and wanted to know what the most difficult part of the game was for me. I told him read-ing defenses and understanding coverages.

"Oh, that's easy. We can teach that!" he said.

Then he asked how could I help an NFL team today. My time with Coach Leonard was literally an interview. He drew up some defenses and explained them to me and had me draw what he just explained. He tested my ability to comprehend different football concepts and plays. The interview went a lot better than I expected; I did really well on his white board test.

"You know, Fendi, basketball and football are very similar. Once you understand football better you can correlate the two and use those basketball skills on the field."

"I look at a player like yourself, and if you work hard, you could be really special. You just have to learn football. If the opportunity presents itself, I'd use bas-ketball terms to teach you."

I thought he was being funny, but he was dead serious.

"Well, Fendi, my work here is done. Good luck this weekend. Hope to see you in the future."

CHAPTER **21**
MY MOMENT

The NFL draft was the next day, and my phone was blowing up! I received so many calls from teams; I had no idea where I was going to end up.

The first call I got was from the Miami Dolphins, followed by the Atlanta Falcons. I also received calls from the Bengals, Jaguars, Cowboys, and Raiders.

This is cra-a-a-a-a-a-zy!

———————

The phone rang. The office lady picked it up.

"Hello? Yes he's all checked in and ready to go. We'll be bringing him in shortly."

We finally left the office, and the lady walked me across a field towards a big house. The first thing I saw was the playground with a basketball court; my eyes lit up!

I hadn't seen a basketball court in so long. I wanted to go play ball right then, but we were walking towards the house.

Is this a foster home or something?

We continued to walk, and I spotted some monkey bars. Then I saw another building that looked like a school over to the left. The lady and I walked through the double doors of the home.

"Hello! This is Fendi Onobun. He'll be spending some time with us."

"Hello Fendi, how are you? I'm Mrs. Nancy, nice to meet you. We'll get you all set up with clothes, shoes, and a room. Okay, sweetie?"

I was so nervous. I didn't know where I was going or who I was going to be with.

"Am I staying here?"

"Yes, sweetie, you'll be staying here for the time being."

My heart dropped.

I had so much anticipation about the draft. I had no clue where I was going to end up and I knew I would drive myself crazy thinking about it.

I left all that to my dad: he had all the write-ups and reports and at least six mock drafts with him. I knew he was just as anxious as I was, if not more.

But everything was in God's hands, and I knew it was going to be OK.

My gut told me told me I'd be a New York Jet or an Oakland Raider; but again, I had no idea. I hadn't heard from New York since I left, and seven new teams had just contacted me that day.

I was confident someone would pick me up, and that was a good feeling.

My dad asked me questions almost every half hour.

"So where do you think you'll end up?"

"Who seemed to like you the most?"

I was just as clueless as he was; I had no idea. My part had been done; it was time to let everything else take care of itself.

Coach Levine gave me a call later that day. "Hey, did you know on this NFL draft scouting website you're considered a top-15 tight end in your class?"

"Really? No, I didn't."

"You have a chance, Fendi, you have a chance. Don't say I didn't tell you so when we first met!" Levine said.

I laughed. "Well, Coach, this is why I did this, so hopefully I can see it come to pass."

"You will. Whether you get drafted or go as a free agent, you're going to get a chance. The more tight ends that get drafted the better. It brings you closer to the top of the list, so lets hope twenty-something tight ends get drafted! You're going to be fine, good luck! Proud of you!"

"Thanks, Coach! I appreciate it!" I told him, and I did appreciate it, very much.

"No problem. Enjoy the moment. Don't stress out!" He said.

The draft started the night of April 22nd, and it was a three-day draft. Only the first round was on day one. Rounds two and three were on day two, and four through seven were done on day three.

I wasn't expecting anything until the third day, but I still wanted to see where some of my friends and these other tight ends would end up. By the end of day two, only five tight ends had been selected.

It wasn't the greatest news, but I remained hopeful. We still had four more rounds left. A little anxiety was setting in. There was no telling how many tight ends would get drafted in the last four rounds.

———

I had been at protective services for a little less than a week. I was given a room and clothes and assigned to a bed.

I was wondering if I was ever going to see my parents again. I was making friends and playing basketball everyday, but I didn't know if I was going to end up with another family as a foster child.

I talked to few of the other kids at the house, and a lot of them were hoping to get adopted. I just wanted to go home to Houston. That wish felt further and further away as the days passed, and there was nothing I could do about it.

We were all on break, so I hadn't been to school yet. Tomorrow was going to be my first day. I was excited and nervous all at the same time, but I was ready.

The following morning I was up early getting dressed with the rest of the boys in our bunk. I didn't know exactly where I was going, but I followed the crowd out of the double doors after breakfast.

We walked over to the school. I wondered who my teacher would be and which classroom I would be going to. No one told me anything.

When we got there, I looked around in confusion, wondering which classroom to walk into. I walked into the one closest to my left and took a seat at a table.

Mrs. Nancy walked in a few seconds later.

"Fendi, come with me." She came walking towards me.

"He's a temp," I heard her tell the teacher. "He's a temp."

I guessed I was in the wrong classroom.

"Come with me, sweetheart."

April 24th had finally come, day three of the NFL draft! I could barely sleep the night before. I knew by the end of the day I'd be on an NFL team.

The big question was where would I end up? It was crazy to imagine this moment. Football came out of nowhere; now I'm awaiting a phone call that's going to forever change my life!

It had only been a year. I couldn't believe it; it was something only God could script. It definitely made all of the reservations, disappointments, and questions I had well worth it.

Today, I'm sitting as an NFL draft hopeful. I felt like I was dreaming.

I went to get breakfast with some friends so I could get my mind off the draft a bit. I didn't want to sit at home and watch every pick from the fourth round on; I knew it would drive me crazy.

Keith kept me updated on picks via text, so I had an idea of where guys were going.

During the fourth round, four more tight ends were selected. Seven total had been drafted. By the time I finished breakfast and got home, it was around the middle of the fifth round.

My phone had not rung yet but I knew the more tight ends selected, the better it was for me.

The fifth round was coming to an end, and I told myself I would watch the sixth and seventh rounds seriously. I was projected to be a late-round pick.

I had my phone by my side, patiently waiting for it to ring. Twelve tight ends had already been drafted, so I was hoping I would hear my name soon.

The sixth round was up next.

———————————

Mrs. Nancy and I started walking back towards the CPS house.

"You're temporary, Fendi you weren't supposed to go to school today. I'm sorry no one told you."

Mrs. Nancy and I were holding hands walking back across the field towards the house.

I looked over to my right and saw a gentleman walking towards the CPS office. He had on a purple and green sweater; a sweater that looked very familiar to me.

"Hey, that guy looks like my dad!" I told Mrs. Nancy.

I looked again: it *was* my dad!

"DADDY!!"

I pulled away from her hand and bolted towards my dad. Running and screaming at the top of my lungs,

I jumped into his arms and gave him the biggest hug I had ever given anyone.

I couldn't believe I was actually seeing my dad!

It was a dream come true.

Reunited back with my dad for the first time in 3 months. January 1994

Just as I was about to watch the start of the sixth round, my phone started to buzz.

My phone's ringing, my phone's ringing!

It was a 314 area code.

"Hello?" I said, trying to remain calm.

"Hi. May I speak to Fendi Onobun?"

My dad and I at the Hoover Dam. After leaving Child Protective Services. January 1994.

"Speaking…"

"Fendi, this is the St. Louis Rams. You're going to be our sixth round pick!"

I had the biggest smile on my face. It was hard to hear everything the representative was saying because I was so excited about the news she had just delivered.

"Make sure you got the TV on so you can watch your name across the screen."

"Yes ma'am!"

I ran into the living room and screamed at the top of my lungs in excitement.

"I'M GOING TO BE A RAM, I'M GOING TO BE A ST. LOUIS RAM!"

My dad was overjoyed! "The Rams! Wow!"

"Yes!" I shouted in delight. "It's about to be on TV, right now!"

We turned our eyes to the television.

St. Louis – PICK IS IN.

We waited, holding our breath in silence.

Round 6. Pick 170 Rams Select FENDI ONOBUN/ TE HOUSTON

April 24, 2010 (Draft Day)
Dad, me, and my stepmom Jolly.

"OH MY GOD!" My dad jumped up and hugged me with tears of joy in the middle of the living room. We were so happy.

"I did it, Dad! I did it! I made it to the NFL!"

My dream had come true.

My family was so excited about the news when they heard. Jolly, my stepmom, was praising God like no other, and my little brothers Miles and Noel were ecstatic: their big brother had just been drafted into the NFL.

I just accomplished my unthinkable goal. In one year, I had made the transition from college basketball to the NFL. I had been working so hard for this moment. It was something I committed to, something I believed I could do.

Hugging my dad in that precious moment took me back to that moment he rescued me from child protective services in 94'. I was seven years old then, without a friend in the world and I didn't know if I'd ever see him again.

My dad fought so hard to get me back, the way I fought to make it to the NFL. He believed he would see his son again, like I believed I'd someday be in the NFL. We had fought for our moments but the joy we shared in *this* moment was indescribable and well worth it. One decision he made to get me back changed the trajectory of my life

My dad had put me into basketball as a kid to help me recover from the trauma of Las Vegas. I had fallen in love with the sport and the rest was history. But football? I pushed for this one, and worked harder than I had ever worked before.

It wasn't my first love, and it didn't come easi-ly but I didn't give up, I committed to something I believed I could do and made it happen. I had loy-al friends and coaches who supported me and helped me to truly believe it would come to pass.

Life is full of swift tran-sitions. I believe God has a way of revealing the meaning of those critical life-changing moments to us. Sometimes we don't

Me in 1995 (8 years old). Houston, Texas.

Me in 2010 (23 years old). St. Louis, Missouri. *Photo Courtesy of the Los Angeles Rams*

**Rookie year with the St. Louis
Rams. 2010-2011 season.**

*Photo courtesy of the Los Angeles
Rams*

know why we go through the experiences we do, but He works in mysterious ways.

From my childhood to this moment, I didn't understand why I had experienced such a rollercoaster ride of fears and faith, rejection and rewards. But He brought everything full circle.

It started where I thought it ended. When the basketball door shut for me at Arizona, it was only the beginning. When I went missing from my dad, it was only the start of a great ending, and I truly thank God for him.

Everyone in the house on draft night was elated. It was such a special time, there were really no words for the feeling. I still couldn't believe it.

"I did it Dad! I made it! I'm a St. Louis Ram."

"I'm proud of you, Fendi, so proud!" He gave me a big hug. "*WOW SON!* You *did* do it! Welcome to the NFL!"

Rookie year with the St. Louis Rams. 2010-2011 season.
Photo courtesy of the Los Angeles Rams

EPILOGUE

I was released from the hospital hours after my knee surgery. It was my second knee operation in four months from a tear I suffered in the NFL with the Jacksonville Jaguars going into my fourth season. This injury is what eventually ended my playing career.

Basketball was by far my first love, and the sport played an instrumental part in my life. The dream I had in the hospital took me back to where it all started and reminded me of the game I loved so much as a kid.

From the recovery room, I began to think about how basketball, football, and my childhood all played such important parts in making me into the person I am today. Bit-by-bit, I started to shed light on my childhood and understand how certain experiences crossed into my adolescent life and then my adult life.

My biological mother kidnapped me when I was seven. Avoiding divorce and custody battles, she decided to flee with me, her only son, and move to Las Vegas, Nevada, in November of 1993.

My dad had to hire a team of private investigators and lawyers to find out where his son and wife had disappeared to. It was a three and a half-month search for my dad and his team.

He wiped out his entire 401k to pay for the expenses involved in finding me. At the time, I was just a little boy, and I had no idea what was going on. But from the second my biological mother Dee told me to pack more than what was necessary for our beach trip, I sensed that something was fishy.

She told many lies and stories to avoid questions about my dad.

My mother and I were moving almost weekly to avoid being caught. I lived at five or six different places during my time in Las Vegas. After months of hiding, my mother was confronted by police.

She had to take them to where I was, and that's where the two lead investigators took me from the apartment and transported me to child protective services. While I was there, my mom and dad dueled it out in court.

I thought CPS was the end for me. I wasn't aware that I was there on a temporary basis. I thought I'd never see my dad or my mom again. I thought I'd be up for adoption shortly after I arrived there.

My father filed for the divorce in Las Vegas and won the custody of me. That was when I saw him at CPS, walking to the office to pick me up.

When we got back to Houston, he signed me up to play in competitive basketball leagues to help cope with the traumatic experience I had just endured. He initially put me into a variety of sports such as tennis, swimming, and soccer, but basketball was my clear favorite.

That was when I truly developed a love for the game. I was always playing it, and as I took more of a liking to it, dad continued to put me in leagues. Basketball was my ticket to a better education, with an opportunity to experience the greatest things life has to offer through sport.

Along the way, friends introduced me to football, and I was blessed to play four seasons in the NFL before my career ended with the Jacksonville Jaguars in 2014.

As for my mother, I do not have a relationship with her. After a seventeen-year break, I have seen her since the kidnapping, but we do not communicate. We did get a chance to speak about what took place, and I am at peace.

I pray all is well with her, and I hold no ill will towards my mother. In spite of what happened, my dad never pressed charges towards Dee, nor did he ever say one bad thing to me about her.

I'm thankful God has blessed me with great people in my life who helped me find ways to overcome the challenges I faced at home and in sports.

If it hadn't been for those good, strong individuals, I wouldn't be where I am today.

I am thankful that God put each of them into my life.

And I am thankful that, with God's help, dreams do come true.

ACKNOWLEDGEMENTS

Special thanks to my wife Stephanie Onobun—
Thank you so much for your unwavering support
throughout this process!

I would also like to thank,

Jolly Onobun
Noel & Miles Onobun
The Rosenblatt Family
Billy & Megan Seymour
Coach Lute Olson
Coach Russ Pennell
Jim Krumpos
Coach Corey Edmond
Lisa Napoleon
Jon Demeter
Kelly Hooker
David Griffin
Doug Gotcher
Coach Sean Miller
Coach James Whitford
Cheryl & Malcolm Tears
The Sawyer Family
Coach Tony Levine

David Griffin
Maria Peden
Coach Kevin Sumlin
Coach Larry Jackson
Coach Chad Dennis
Mike "Doc" O'Shea
Tyron Carrier
James Cleveland
Mikado Hinson
Alonzo Highsmith
Jerry Rhome
Coach David Sloan
Joel Nass
Steve Feeks

You all played an instrumental part throughout this story. I want to say I truly appreciate your help along the way. Thank you again. God Bless!